The U.S. Marine Corps

KNOW YOUR GOVERNMENT

The U.S. Marine Corps

Jack Rummel

CHELSEA HOUSE PUBLISHERS

On the cover: Marines charge ashore from their landing craft during a practice maneuver at Camp Lejeune, North Carolina, in May 1987.
Frontispiece: A marine poses in an amphibious tractor at training exercises on Iwo Jima in 1982. The amphibious tractor, or amtrack, can operate both on land and at sea, thus eliminating the need for the marines to wade through water.

Chelsea House Publishers
Editor-in-Chief: Nancy Toff
Executive Editor: Remmel T. Nunn
Managing Editor: Karyn Gullen Browne
Copy Chief: Juliann Barbato
Picture Editor: Adrian G. Allen
Art Director: Maria Epes
Manufacturing Manager: Gerald Levine

Know Your Government
Senior Editor: Kathy Kuhtz

Staff for THE U.S. MARINE CORPS
Assistant Editor: Karen Schimmel
Copy Editor: Brian Sookram
Deputy Copy Chief: Nicole Bowen
Editorial Assistant: Elizabeth Nix
Picture Researcher: Dixon & Turner Research Associates, Inc.; Joann Stern
Picture Coordinator: Melanie Sanford
Assistant Art Director: Loraine Machlin
Senior Designer: Noreen M. Lamb
Production Manager: Joseph Romano
Production Coordinator: Marie Claire Cebrián

3 5 7 9 8 6 4 2

Library of Congress Cataloging-in-Publication Data

Rummel, Jack.
   The U.S. Marine Corps / Jack Rummel.
      p.   cm.—(Know your government)
   Bibliography: p.
   Includes index.
   ISBN 1-55546-110-7
         0-7910-0910-6 (pbk.)
   1. United States. Marine Corps.   I. Title.   II. Series: Know
your government (New York, N.Y.)
VE23.R86   1990   89-10025
359.9'6'0973—dc20   CIP

95- 4139
J
359.9
Rum
YA

CONTENTS

KNOW YOUR GOVERNMENT

The American Red Cross
The Bureau of Indian Affairs
The Central Intelligence Agency
The Commission on Civil Rights
The Department of Agriculture
The Department of the Air Force
The Department of the Army
The Department of Commerce
The Department of Defense
The Department of Education
The Department of Energy
The Department of Health and
  Human Services
The Department of Housing and
  Urban Development
The Department of the Interior
The Department of Justice
The Department of Labor
The Department of the Navy
The Department of State
The Department of Transportation
The Department of the Treasury
The Drug Enforcement Administration
The Environmental Protection Agency
The Equal Employment
  Opportunities Commission
The Federal Aviation Administration
The Federal Bureau of Investigation
The Federal Communications Commission
The Federal Government: How it Works
The Federal Reserve System
The Federal Trade Commission
The Food and Drug Administration
The Forest Service

The House of Representatives
The Immigration and Naturalization Service
The Internal Revenue Service
The Library of Congress
The National Aeronautics and Space
  Administration
The National Archives and Records
  Administration
The National Foundation on the Arts
  and the Humanities
The National Park Service
The National Science Foundation
The Nuclear Regulatory Commission
The Peace Corps
The Presidency
The Public Health Service
The Securities and Exchange Commission
The Senate
The Small Business Administration
The Smithsonian
The Supreme Court
The Tennessee Valley Authority
The U.S. Arms Control and
  Disarmament Agency
The U.S. Coast Guard
The U.S. Constitution
The U.S. Fish and Wildlife Service
The U.S. Information Agency
The U.S. Marine Corps
The U.S. Mint
The U.S. Postal Service
The U.S. Secret Service
The Veterans Administration

CHELSEA HOUSE PUBLISHERS

INTRODUCTION

Government: Crises of Confidence

Arthur M. Schlesinger, jr.

From the start, Americans have regarded their government with a mixture of reliance and mistrust. The men who founded the republic did not doubt the indispensability of government. "If men were angels," observed the 51st Federalist Paper, "no government would be necessary." But men are not angels. Because human beings are subject to wicked as well as to noble impulses, government was deemed essential to assure freedom and order.

At the same time, the American revolutionaries knew that government could also become a source of injury and oppression. The men who gathered in Philadelphia in 1787 to write the Constitution therefore had two purposes in mind. They wanted to establish a strong central authority and to limit that central authority's capacity to abuse its power.

To prevent the abuse of power, the Founding Fathers wrote two basic principles into the new Constitution. The principle of federalism divided power between the state governments and the central authority. The principle of the separation of powers subdivided the central authority itself into three branches—the executive, the legislative, and the judiciary—so that "each may be a check on the other." The *Know Your Government* series focuses on the major executive departments and agencies in these branches of the federal government.

The Constitution did not plan the executive branch in any detail. After vesting the executive power in the president, it assumed the existence of "executive departments" without specifying what these departments should be. Congress began defining their functions in 1789 by creating the Departments of State, Treasury, and War. The secretaries in charge of these departments made up President Washington's first cabinet. Congress also provided for a legal officer, and President Washington soon invited the attorney general, as he was called, to attend cabinet meetings. As need required, Congress created more executive departments.

Setting up the cabinet was only the first step in organizing the American state. With almost no guidance from the Constitution, President Washington, seconded by Alexander Hamilton, his brilliant secretary of the treasury, equipped the infant republic with a working administrative structure. The Federalists believed in both executive energy and executive accountability and set high standards for public appointments. The Jeffersonian opposition had less faith in strong government and preferred local government to the central authority. But when Jefferson himself became president in 1801, although he set out to change the direction of policy, he found no reason to alter the framework the Federalists had erected.

By 1801 there were about 3,000 federal civilian employees in a nation of a little more than 5 million people. Growth in territory and population steadily enlarged national responsibilities. Thirty years later, when Jackson was president, there were more than 11,000 government workers in a nation of 13 million. The federal establishment was increasing at a faster rate than the population.

Jackson's presidency brought significant changes in the federal service. He believed that the executive branch contained too many officials who saw their jobs as "species of property" and as "a means of promoting individual interest." Against the idea of a permanent service based on life tenure, Jackson argued for the periodic redistribution of federal offices, contending that this was the democratic way and that official duties could be made "so plain and simple that men of intelligence may readily qualify themselves for their performance." He called this policy rotation-in-office. His opponents called it the spoils system.

In fact, partisan legend exaggerated the extent of Jackson's removals. More than 80 percent of federal officeholders retained their jobs. Jackson discharged no larger a proportion of government workers than Jefferson had done a generation earlier. But the rise in these years of mass political parties gave federal patronage new importance as a means of building the party and of rewarding activists. Jackson's successors were less restrained in the distribution of spoils. As the federal establishment grew—to nearly 40,000 by 1861—the politicization of the public service excited increasing concern.

After the Civil War the spoils system became a major political issue. High-minded men condemned it as the root of all political evil. The spoilsmen, said the British commentator James Bryce, "have distorted and depraved the mechanism of politics." Patronage, by giving jobs to unqualified, incompetent, and dishonest persons, lowered the standards of public service and nourished corrupt political machines. Office-seekers pursued presidents and cabinet secretaries without mercy. "Patronage," said Ulysses S. Grant after his presidency, "is the bane of the presidential office." "Every time I appoint someone to office," said another political leader, "I make a hundred enemies and one ingrate." George William Curtis, the president of the National Civil Service Reform League, summed up the indictment. He said,

> The theory which perverts public trusts into party spoils, making public
> employment dependent upon personal favor and not on proved merit,
> necessarily ruins the self-respect of public employees, destroys the
> function of party in a republic, prostitutes elections into a desperate
> strife for personal profit, and degrades the national character by lower-
> ing the moral tone and standard of the country.

The object of civil service reform was to promote efficiency and honesty in the public service and to bring about the ethical regeneration of public life. Over bitter opposition from politicians, the reformers in 1883 passed the Pendleton Act, establishing a bipartisan Civil Service Commission, competitive examinations, and appointment on merit. The Pendleton Act also gave the president authority to extend by executive order the number of "classified" jobs—that is, jobs subject to the merit system. The act applied initially only to about 14,000 of the more than 100,000 federal positions. But by the end of the 19th century 40 percent of federal jobs had moved into the classified category.

Civil service reform was in part a response to the growing complexity of American life. As society grew more organized and problems more technical, official duties were no longer so plain and simple that any person of intelligence could perform them. In public service, as in other areas, the all-round man was yielding ground to the expert, the amateur to the professional. The excesses of the spoils system thus provoked the counter-ideal of scientific public administration, separate from politics and, as far as possible, insulated against it.

The cult of the expert, however, had its own excesses. The idea that administration could be divorced from policy was an illusion. And in the realm of policy, the expert, however much segregated from partisan politics, can

9

never attain perfect objectivity. He remains the prisoner of his own set of values. It is these values rather than technical expertise that determine fundamental judgments of public policy. To turn over such judgments to experts, moreover, would be to abandon democracy itself; for in a democracy final decisions must be made by the people and their elected representatives. "The business of the expert," the British political scientist Harold Laski rightly said, "is to be on tap and not on top."

Politics, however, were deeply ingrained in American folkways. This meant intermittent tension between the presidential government, elected every four years by the people, and the permanent government, which saw presidents come and go while it went on forever. Sometimes the permanent government knew better than its political masters; sometimes it opposed or sabotaged valuable new initiatives. In the end a strong president with effective cabinet secretaries could make the permanent government responsive to presidential purpose, but it was often an exasperating struggle.

The struggle within the executive branch was less important, however, than the growing impatience with bureaucracy in society as a whole. The 20th century saw a considerable expansion of the federal establishment. The Great Depression and the New Deal led the national government to take on a variety of new responsibilities. The New Deal extended the federal regulatory apparatus. By 1940, in a nation of 130 million people, the number of federal workers for the first time passed the 1 million mark. The Second World War brought federal civilian employment to 3.8 million in 1945. With peace, the federal establishment declined to around 2 million by 1950. Then growth resumed, reaching 2.8 million by the 1980s.

The New Deal years saw rising criticism of "big government" and "bureaucracy." Businessmen resented federal regulation. Conservatives worried about the impact of paternalistic government on individual self-reliance, on community responsibility, and on economic and personal freedom. The nation in effect renewed the old debate between Hamilton and Jefferson in the early republic, although with an ironic exchange of positions. For the Hamiltonian constituency, the "rich and well-born," once the advocate of affirmative government, now condemned government intervention, while the Jeffersonian constituency, the plain people, once the advocate of a weak central government and of states' rights, now favored government intervention.

In the 1980s, with the presidency of Ronald Reagan, the debate has burst out with unusual intensity. According to conservatives, government intervention abridges liberty, stifles enterprise, and is inefficient, wasteful, and arbitrary. It disturbs the harmony of the self-adjusting market and creates worse troubles than it solves. Get government off our backs, according to the popular cliché, and our problems will solve themselves. When government is necessary, let it be at the local level, close to the people. Above all, stop the inexorable growth of the federal government.

In fact, for all the talk about the "swollen" and "bloated" bureaucracy, the federal establishment has not been growing as inexorably as many Americans seem to believe. In 1949, it consisted of 2.1 million people. Thirty years later, while the country had grown by 70 million, the federal force had grown only by 750,000. Federal workers were a smaller percentage of the population in 1985 than they were in 1955—or in 1940. The federal establishment, in short, has not kept pace with population growth. Moreover, national defense and the postal service account for 60 percent of federal employment.

Why then the widespread idea about the remorseless growth of government? It is partly because in the 1960s the national government assumed new and intrusive functions: affirmative action in civil rights, environmental protection, safety and health in the workplace, community organization, legal aid to the poor. Although this enlargement of the federal regulatory role was accompanied by marked growth in the size of government on all levels, the expansion has taken place primarily in state and local government. Whereas the federal force increased by only 27 percent in the 30 years after 1950, the state and local government force increased by an astonishing 212 percent.

Despite the statistics, the conviction flourishes in some minds that the national government is a steadily growing behemoth swallowing up the liberties of the people. The foes of Washington prefer local government, feeling it is closer to the people and therefore allegedly more responsive to popular needs. Obviously there is a great deal to be said for settling local questions locally. But local government is characteristically the government of the locally powerful. Historically, the way the locally powerless have won their human and constitutional rights has often been through appeal to the national government. The national government has vindicated racial justice against local bigotry, defended the Bill of Rights against local vigilantism, and protected natural resources against local greed. It has civilized industry and secured the rights of labor organizations. Had the states' rights creed prevailed, there would perhaps still be slavery in the United States.

The national authority, far from diminishing the individual, has given most Americans more personal dignity and liberty than ever before. The individual freedoms destroyed by the increase in national authority have been in the main the freedom to deny black Americans their rights as citizens; the freedom to put small children to work in mills and immigrants in sweatshops; the freedom to pay starvation wages, require barbarous working hours, and permit squalid working conditions; the freedom to deceive in the sale of goods and securities; the freedom to pollute the environment—all freedoms that, one supposes, a civilized nation can readily do without.

"Statements are made," said President John F. Kennedy in 1963, "labelling the Federal Government an outsider, an intruder, an adversary. . . . The United States Government is not a stranger or not an enemy. It is the people of fifty states joining in a national effort. . . . Only a great national effort by a great people working together can explore the mysteries of space, harvest the products at the bottom of the ocean, and mobilize the human, natural, and material resources of our lands."

So an old debate continues. However, Americans are of two minds. When pollsters ask large, spacious questions—Do you think government has become too involved in your lives? Do you think government should stop regulating business?—a sizable majority opposes big government. But when asked specific questions about the practical work of government—Do you favor social security? unemployment compensation? Medicare? health and safety standards in factories? environmental protection? government guarantee of jobs for everyone seeking employment? price and wage controls when inflation threatens?—a sizable majority approves of intervention.

In general, Americans do not want less government. What they want is more efficient government. They want government to do a better job. For a time in the 1970s, with Vietnam and Watergate, Americans lost confidence in the national government. In 1964, more than three-quarters of those polled had thought the national government could be trusted to do right most of the time. By 1980 only one-quarter was prepared to offer such trust. But by 1984 trust in the federal government to manage national affairs had climbed back to 45 percent.

Bureaucracy is a term of abuse. But it is impossible to run any large organization, whether public or private, without a bureaucracy's division of labor and hierarchy of authority. And we live in a world of large organizations. Without bureaucracy modern society would collapse. The problem is not to abolish bureaucracy, but to make it flexible, efficient, and capable of innovation.

Two hundred years after the drafting of the Constitution, Americans still regard government with a mixture of reliance and mistrust—a good combination. Mistrust is the best way to keep government reliable. Informed criticism is the means of correcting governmental inefficiency, incompetence, and arbitrariness; that is, of best enabling government to play its essential role. For without government, we cannot attain the goals of the Founding Fathers. Without an understanding of government, we cannot have the informed criticism that makes government do the job right. It is the duty of every American citizen to know our government—which is what this series is all about.

*In February 1984 a marine of the Twenty-second Marine Amphibious Unit
waits to return to his squadron after concluding a multinational peacekeeping operation in Beirut, Lebanon. The Marine Corps is considered to be an
elite fighting force of highly motivated and well-disciplined volunteers.*

ONE

Always Faithful

Early on the morning of October 23, 1983, a yellow Mercedes truck laden with several hundred pounds of explosives crashed through a flimsy barrier at the entrance of the Twenty-fourth Marine Amphibious Unit's temporary barracks in Beirut, Lebanon. Caught by surprise, the marine guards posted at the gate were unable to stop the lone intruder. The driver steered the truck straight into the barracks and pushed an electronic button that detonated his cargo. The explosion leveled the four-story building.

Two hundred twenty marines, 18 navy men, and 3 soldiers died in the attack that morning, and more than 60 marines were wounded. Other Marine Corps units stationed at the Beirut airport rushed to the barracks and worked frantically throughout the day and night to dig out their dead and injured comrades. The most severely hurt were immediately flown to the U.S. military hospital in Wiesbaden, West Germany. It was the Marine Corps's worst single disaster in terms of loss of life since the end of World War II in 1945.

Word of the bombing shocked officials in Washington, D.C., and Americans throughout the United States. The 1,800 men of the amphibious unit had been ordered to faraway Beirut by their commander in chief, President Ronald Reagan. As part of a three-nation international peacekeeping force, the marines' job was to guard the Beirut airport and to maintain a presence in and around southern Beirut. Violent clashes between the many warring factions vying for power in the strife-torn country had brought the marines to Lebanon in 1982. Although they are known mainly for fighting wars rather than preventing them, peacekeeping was not an entirely new role for the marines. They had been sent as peacekeepers to Lebanon once before, by President Dwight Eisenhower in 1958, and small units of marines had helped in peaceful missions to rescue flood and earthquake victims in Morocco, Ceylon, and Spain during the 1950s and 1960s.

The commandant of the Marine Corps, General P. X. Kelley, quickly flew to Beirut to reassure his troops and to assess how the intruder had managed to get into the marine compound. He also hoped to gain information that would help prevent such attacks in the future. But before he landed in the Lebanese capital, Kelley stopped at the military hospital in Wiesbaden.

The bond between a commanding officer and his troops is one of the essential elements that makes for an effective fighting—or peacekeeping—force. It was unthinkable to General Kelley to visit the remaining marines in

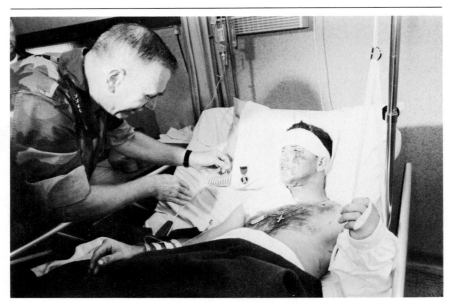

On October 24, 1983, General P. X. Kelley, commandant of the Marine Corps, visits a marine who was injured when a terrorist bomb destroyed the marine barracks in Beirut, Lebanon. General Kelley's visit to the Wiesbaden military hospital in West Germany, where the wounded had been taken, epitomizes the strong bond that exists between a commanding officer and his troops.

16

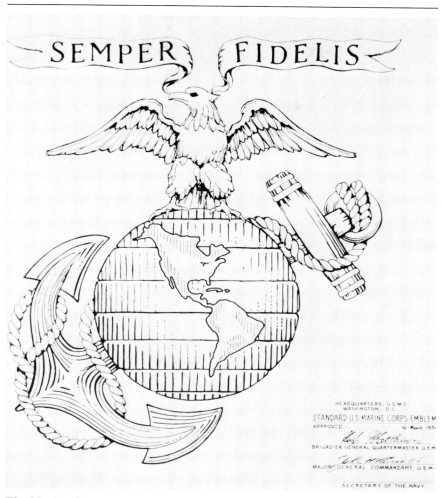

SEMPER FIDELIS

The Marine Corps emblem—an eagle, a globe, and an anchor—bears the motto Semper fidelis, *"always faithful." The marines' extraordinary fighting spirit and faithfulness to each other have made the corps stand out from the other armed services.*

Beirut without also going to Wiesbaden to visit those who had been wounded. Kelley walked among the beds of his injured troops, offering consolation and pinning the Purple Heart—the medal given to those who have been wounded in combat—onto the hospital gowns of the fallen marines. Among these men was Lance Corporal Jeffrey Nashton of Rome, New York. Kelley had arrived in Wiesbaden less than 24 hours after the blast, and Nashton was still in critical condition. "He had every life support device imaginable on him," General Kelley later said. "When I went in to talk to him and introduced myself, he could not see very well. The young marine reached up, clutched my four stars and counted them just to make sure that I was who I said I was. Then he tried to write on the sheet with his finger. None of us could make heads or tails out of what he was saying. Then the nurse gave him a pad and a pencil, and he wrote 'Semper Fi.' "

Semper fi is an abbreviation of the Latin phrase *semper fidelis*, the Marine Corps motto. It means "always faithful" and in two simple words sums up the tradition of service to country of the United States Marine Corps.

Throughout its history the Marine Corps has been an elite fighting force of volunteers. Unlike the army and the navy, the Marine Corps seldom has resorted to the draft to fill its ranks. Because of this ready-and-willing fighting tradition the corps has earned a reputation as a highly motivated, well-disciplined fighting group.

Smaller and less influential than the army and the navy (and later the air force), the Marine Corps's tremendous fighting spirit and the "faithfulness" of marines to each other have made the corps stand out from the other services. This is what Lance Corporal Nashton was alluding to when he scratched the words *Semper Fi* on the notepad for General Kelley that day in West Germany.

Amphibious Force: The Fighting Sailors

The U.S. Marine Corps began its history in the war of independence that was fought between the 13 American colonies and the premier imperial power of the 18th century, Great Britain. The corps was created during this war because its troops served the useful role of seaborne soldiers. Although the army's role has always been to fight large land battles in defense of the nation—and the navy has been charged with the responsibility of fighting on the oceans of the world—the marines began with a smaller, more narrow niche in the American defense scheme.

The first marines were volunteer sailors and fishermen who attacked British merchant ships whenever they could do so with a reasonable assurance of victory. During the revolutionary war and the early days of the American republic the marines were used primarily as fighting forces carried aboard American ships. They were charged with defending sailing vessels from attack by enemy ships and marines and with storming and taking enemy naval and

Marines attack a British ship in 1776. During the revolutionary war the marines were used as fighting forces carried aboard U.S. Navy ships: They were charged with defending naval vessels from enemy attack and with overtaking the enemy by lashing the ships together, storming the opponent's ship, and engaging in hand-to-hand combat.

merchant vessels. After the United States Marine Corps was formally organized in 1798, marines were found aboard all ships of the U.S. Navy, where, besides their other duties, they manned cannons and kept order on board. Furthermore, in the 18th and early 19th centuries marines frequently were required to climb up the sail riggings and fire down on the crews of enemy ships with muskets and pistols. In addition, they operated small cannons loaded with iron shot about the size of grapes (appropriately called grapeshot), which were fired from one ship across the deck of another. The marines were expected to lash ships together in close-quarter fights and storm onto their adversary's ship, engaging in hand-to-hand combat with opposing marines and sailors. This was the way many sea battles were fought during that time. Outright sinking of another ship by cannon fire was comparatively rare.

Another task delegated to the marines during the 18th and early 19th centuries was to attack coastal towns and fortifications. Typically, marines would be landed from a ship to storm a fort guarding a port—or to seize the port town itself. These engagements did not last long, as the marines were not usually a large enough force to take and hold a major town against a land-based army. These hit-and-run tactics worked very well against the French and British in the Caribbean and the Barbary Arabs in the Mediterranean. But because the marines were seen primarily as a force used in naval warfare, they were viewed as an arm of the navy and operated in the navy's shadow.

The Marine Corps's position within the U.S. military structure reflected this view. The commandant of the Marine Corps reported to the secretary of the navy, who in turn was subordinate to the secretary of war, a cabinet-level civilian official appointed by the president. With the exception of name and rank changes for some of the offices, this structure remains basically the same today.

From Square Riggers to Attack Helicopters

Two developments changed the marines' role over the next 200 years: the growth and expansion of the United States—and its influence throughout the world—and the tremendous technological change experienced in the 19th and 20th centuries. American power and prestige grew rapidly after the Civil War (1861–65) because of the industrialization and commercial expansion that occurred in the United States. As a result of its new strength and world position, the U.S. government felt that it had the obligation and the right to intervene in the crises that periodically erupted in different parts of the world.

The U.S. Marine Guard on board the USS Kearsarge *during the Civil War. The primary mission of the corps during the war was to help blockade Southern ports in order to stop all seaborne traffic and communications to and from the South.*

The United States now saw itself as equal to the great European imperial powers and in many ways began to copy the behavior of these countries. Part of this behavior involved military intervention in the affairs of other nations. Because they were more or less constantly on call aboard the ships of the U.S. Navy, the marines were the force most frequently depended on to meet these crises. By the 1920s they had been sent to places many Americans had never heard of: Panama, Nicaragua, the Philippines, Peking (now called Beijing), Haiti, and Japan, among others.

The role of the marines has crested and ebbed with technological innovation. For many years after the Civil War the purpose—even the relevance—of the corps was uncertain, owing to rapid changes being made in ship design and construction. When large, accurate guns were placed on steam-driven, steel-hulled boats in the mid-19th century marines found themselves unable to storm enemy vessels because enhanced firepower no longer required large ships to fight close to each other. Other changes that dramatically altered the way wars were fought followed one after the other: the invention of the airplane and the submarine, the introduction of chemical weapons, the appearance of helicopters and jet airplanes, the atomic bomb, and the development of

U.S. Marines, fighting in the swamps of northwestern South Vietnam, call for air support in 1966. A year earlier, two battalions of marines had been sent to Da Nang to defend an airfield there, becoming the first American combat troops in Vietnam. When the United States has needed a rapid military response to events anywhere in the world, the Marine Corps has always been prepared to respond.

space-based electronic/laser warfare (sometimes referred to as "Star Wars" technology). Each of these new inventions has affected the Marine Corps. And each has prompted critics to ask whether or not the corps has become obsolete. Time and again the Marine Corps has risen to the challenge offered by the changing nature of the U.S. military establishment. The reason it has survived for so long is basic: When the United States has needed a rapid military response to events anywhere in the world, the Marine Corps has always been ready to respond. It has been able to quickly transport highly motivated marines to trouble spots. And so far, no new invention has replaced a man armed with a rifle as the basic instrument needed to win a battle or a war.

The history of the U.S. Marine Corps is not without controversy. The corps has been involved in some military engagements that have aroused protest and criticism from the very citizens in whose name its troops have fought. This criticism has been especially loud when the marines have been used to intervene in Latin America and Asia. In such instances the Marine Corps has been viewed by many in the United States and abroad as an instrument of American imperialism. In some of these cases, rather than being praised as an army of liberation, the marines have been criticized as an army of occupation whose purpose is to oppress the people of poor and militarily weak countries.

Regardless of the opinion of the marines' role in world affairs, it cannot be disputed that the Marine Corps is at the disposal of American civilian leaders. Any fighting in which the corps is involved is the result of the order of the president of the United States, who is elected by the American people. Ultimately, all Americans share the blame—and the glory—of the actions of the U.S. Marines. Like most people, they are not perfect, but they are essentially honorable and decent. The history of the Marine Corps is long and interesting, and it can tell us a great deal about the evolution of the United States—and about what it means to be an American in a world of competing countries with conflicting interests.

The uniform worn by the Continental marines from 1779 to 1783. When the revolutionary war began in 1775, the marines' green coat was trimmed with white.

TWO

To the Shores
of Tripoli

Initially the groups that later became the U.S. Marine Corps were little more than small, ragtag bands of fighting sailors from the coastal towns of the Atlantic seaboard. In 1775, during the initial heady days of the Revolution, American fishermen, sailors, and merchant-traders volunteered for service as naval fighting men. These first marines, who were organized into scattered fighting forces under separate commands, were active in 11 of the original 13 colonies. The group that engaged in the most fighting during this early period was a band of fishermen from Marblehead, Massachusetts, who harassed the British navy during George Washington's siege of Boston in the fall of 1775. Other raiding parties were made up of privateers—privately owned ships fitted with cannons, the owners of which were issued letters of marque by the government, allowing them to seize goods or people carried on enemy ships in retaliation for past injuries. These ships operated out of Philadelphia and small ports along the coast of New Jersey and the Carolinas, as well as up the Delaware and Chesapeake bays.

Often the lure for the crews of these ships was as much financial as patriotic. Many owners of privateers became rich during the American Revolution as a result of the cargo they captured from British merchant ships. Common crewmen and marines frequently received a share of the captured loot. This kind of raiding was permitted by the American revolutionary government and was an effective way to disrupt the supplies on which the British army was dependent.

By late 1775 American revolutionary leaders realized that a more organized and united fighting force was necessary to press the struggle against the British government. American leaders had only to study the success of their enemy to know the value of soldiers carried aboard ships. The British had long employed their Royal Marines as a weapon of their imperial policy. George Washington's half brother, Lawrence, had served in a regiment of the Royal Marines that raided Cartagena, the rich Spanish port on the Caribbean coast of South America, in 1740. And in 1775, as General Washington besieged Boston, he was faced by a regiment of the Royal Marines who had been deployed from warships in the harbor.

The Revolutionary War

When the Second Continental Congress met in late October 1775 to consider how the American colonies could fight more effectively for their independence, one of its principal actions was to pass a resolution that created the Continental navy and marines. Caucusing in Peg Mullan's Tun Tavern (one of Philadelphia's less fashionable inns but nearby the State House, where the Second Continental Congress met as a whole), a group of delegates led by John Adams of Massachusetts worked out the language of a proposal that was adopted by Congress on November 10, 1775:

> Resolved, that two Battalions of Marines be raised consisting of one
> Colonel, two lieutenant Colonels, two Majors & Officers as usual in
> other regiments, that they consist of an equal number of privates
> with other battalions. . . . That they be inlisted and commissioned
> for and during the present war between Great Britain and the colo-
> nies, unless dismissed by order of Congress.

This first group was known as the Continental marines. Like their British counterparts in the Royal Marines, the Continental marines were charged with maintaining order aboard ship, firing muskets and grenades at the crews of other ships during close-quarter sea battles, storming ships at sea, guarding prisoners below deck, and mounting seaborne raids against coastal towns and fortifications.

On November 10, 1775, the Continental Congress passed this resolution authorizing the establishment of two battalions of marines. The marines were charged with maintaining order aboard ship and firing muskets at the crews of enemy ships during close-range sea battles.

American military leaders were never able to raise two battalions of marines during the Revolution. (The total number of marines who served as enlisted men during the war was less than 2,000.) Instead, beginning with Samuel Nicholas, the 32-year-old proprietor of the Conestogoe Waggon inn in Philadelphia, a small force of marines was assembled. A fife-and-drum corps was sent out into the streets of Philadelphia literally to "drum up" volunteers. Nicholas, the first marine officer, was commissioned as a marine captain by John Hancock, the president of the Second Continental Congress, on November 28, 1775.

Meanwhile, gun ports were being sawed into merchant ships so that they could be converted into battleships of the new Continental navy. One of these ships was the *Black Prince*, a merchant sloop that was refitted in Philadelphia by a young Scottish-American named John Paul Jones. This newly renovated warship was then christened the *Alfred* and became the flagship of the American squadron that was preparing to sail out of Philadelphia to confront the powerful Royal Navy. On December 5, 1775, 100 volunteer marines arrived in Philadelphia from Rhode Island. With them was Esek Hopkins, a salty 40-year-old sea captain who would command the American squadron. The squadron, the first American fleet with marines, consisted of the 24-gun *Alfred*, a 20-gun sloop named the *Columbus*, and 6 other ships (the smallest being a 6-gun boat known as the *Fly*). It also included 234 marines organized in 4 companies.

Commodore Hopkins's orders from the Continental Congress were to sweep the British navy from Chesapeake Bay and the North and South Carolina coasts and to "attack, take, and destroy" the enemy in Rhode Island. This was a tall order for an eight-ship squadron that found itself up against a much larger, better-equipped, and centuries-old navy—a navy that, in the 18th century, was arguably the best oceangoing fighting force in the world. Wisely, Hopkins chose a more modest goal.

Claiming to leaders of the Continental Congress that he had been blown off course by the wind (at that time even the British navy was at the mercy of the wind), Hopkins prepared to swoop down on Nassau in the Bahamas, where he would land 200 marines to take the settlement. The commodore's plans called for a surprise attack, but the squadron was discovered before the marines and sailors could land, and they were run off by cannon fire from the fort guarding the town. Hopkins then proceeded to Fort Montagu, a less important prize four miles from Nassau Town. On March 3, 1776, the marines were landed at the fort, and after a short battle they managed to force the surrender of the smaller British force. The marines seized 40 cannons and 15 brass mortars, but they were not able to confiscate a valuable cache of gunpowder, which was spirited away in the night by the British commander. This blunder eventually led the Continental Congress to censure Hopkins and dismiss him from naval service.

Nevertheless, the marines, who were under the direct command of Captain Nicholas, performed bravely and well in their first official action as an organized fighting unit. At a later engagement in Long Island Sound this same force helped seize four small ships and fended off an attack from the British warship *Glasgow*. They were received with a hero's welcome in New London, Connecticut, and Nicholas was promoted to major, with a pay increase to $32 a month. Soon after this, the Continental Congress decreed that the marines should have a uniform: green coats with white trim, a round hat with the left brim pinned to the crown, and a sheath of thick leather (called a stock) buckled around the neck to ward off sword slashes and keep the head of the enlisted man erect. The stock, which was worn by the corps until the Civil War, was more a nuisance than a benefit, but because of it the marines derived a nickname that is still in use: leathernecks.

The Continental marines served with distinction in two other theaters of the War of Independence. The first of these found the marines fighting with General Washington in New Jersey in the winter of 1776. Having been forced off Long Island and chased through northern New Jersey by a large British army commanded by General William Howe, Washington called on Major Nicholas's company for help. Nicholas's marines, now numbering 131 men,

The Continental marines charge into battle against British troops during the revolutionary war. Painted on the marines' drums is a popular phrase of the time, Don't tread on me.

were ferried across the Delaware River and fought an important battle near Princeton, New Jersey, on New Year's Day 1777. Nicholas's additional forces allowed Washington to rout the British and protect the American capital of Philadelphia throughout the rest of the winter.

The other theater of action was the one in which the American marines and navy gained their greatest fame during the War of Independence. Sailing with a squadron of five warships, Captain John Paul Jones sought to bring the war home to the British by raiding Ireland, the North Sea, and England itself in 1778. Setting sail from Portsmouth, New Hampshire, on his flagship *Ranger* in July 1777, Jones journeyed first to France, where he delivered dispatches to Benjamin Franklin, who was then the American envoy in Paris.

In April 1778, after prowling the French coast for several months in search of British merchant ships, Jones took his squadron to the Irish Sea. During the next week and a half his group captured two merchant vessels, sank a Scottish schooner, and engaged in a battle with a British revenue cutter (a small, swift ship designed to intercept smugglers and to help collect customs duties for the government). During this time, Jones was obliged to replace the marine commander, Captain Matthew Pierce, who was a friend of his, with another man favored by the majority of the marines aboard his ships. The new commander, Lieutenant Samuel Wallingford, was a native of Portsmouth, the home port of most of the marines in Jones's squadron, and as a result he was more popular than the original commander. On April 22, Jones attacked Whitehaven, England, a port town on the Irish Sea—but not before he personally put down a mutiny aboard his ship. Some of the men from Portsmouth, afraid that Jones's plan to attack the English port was too reckless, rose in rebellion and tried to overthrow their plucky leader.

The attack on Whitehaven was brazen and successful. Slipping into the port at midnight, Jones dispatched a group of 30 marines in rowboats to take the fort that guarded the harbor. The soldiers stationed at the fort were surprised and quickly defeated, and the fort was captured. Then Jones took the marines into the town itself, where he walked into a tavern to relight his men's torches and proceeded to set fire to a large ship berthed at the wharf. By dawn Jones and the marines had left Whitehaven and were bound for nearby St. Mary's Isle, which was the ancestral home of a British lord, the earl of Selkirk. A detachment of marines with orders to kidnap the earl (he was to be held as hostage and exchanged for American prisoners) stormed the nobleman's house, but he was not there. As compensation, the marines confiscated the lord's family silver. The countess of Selkirk later wrote that among the officers in the raiding party was "a civil young man in a green uniform, an anchor on his

Scottish-born John Paul Jones was one of America's most daring and successful naval officers to fight in the revolutionary war. In the Irish Sea, Jones and the marines and sailors aboard his ships brought the war home to the British by capturing two British merchant vessels, sinking a Scottish schooner, and engaging in a battle with a British revenue cutter.

On September 23, 1779, Captain John Paul Jones and his crew storm the British man-of-war Serapis *after strapping it to the* Bonhomme Richard. *When asked by the British commander if he wanted to surrender, Jones replied, "I have not yet begun to fight." The British were forced to surrender later that night.*

buttons[,] which were white." The marine in the green uniform was Lieutenant Wallingford.

Jones's most famous victory in the European theater of the revolutionary war occurred more than a year later. Having preyed on British merchant ships continuously since the raid on Whitehaven, Jones was well known to the British navy, which listed his capture as a high priority. On September 23, 1779, Jones, in a refurbished ship called the *Bonhomme Richard* (Poor Richard, named after Benjamin Franklin's *Poor Richard's Almanack*), was caught by the larger British man-of-war *Serapis* off Flamborough Head, Yorkshire. A fierce sea battle began at seven in the evening. Jones knew that his only chance for survival lay in staying as close to the other ship as possible and hoping that his mixed crew of French, Irish, and American marines could storm the *Serapis*. The *Bonhomme Richard*'s main guns were blown out quickly by the larger vessel, but Jones's marines managed to strap the two vessels together. Taking water from repeated cannonade, the *Bonhomme Richard* appeared to be sinking. Asked by the British commander if he wanted to surrender, Jones shouted back his famous reply, "I have not yet begun to fight." Somehow, the marines and sailors managed to overcome the odds against them. They took the deck of the *Serapis,* and a seaman tossed a grenade into its hold, setting off an explosion below deck that broke the morale of the British sailors. At 10:30 that night the British ran up the flag of surrender.

The marines fought several more battles before the war effectively ended with the surrender of General Charles Cornwallis at Yorktown, Virginia, in October 1781. But not all of these engagements resulted in victory for the leathernecks.Their last battle of the war, the defense of Charleston, South Carolina, against a British attack, ended in defeat. They were not as yet a solid, experienced fighting unit of professional fighting men. Rather, they were more like a band of citizen-soldiers, gripped with enthusiasm and love of country but short on tradition and *esprit de corps.*

The Barbary Wars

The new government of the United States of America quickly demobilized its armed forces following the War of Independence. Because they had witnessed the ceaseless warfare and intrigue of the European countries, Americans feared both a centralized government and a large standing army. For a while Americans were able to live virtually without an army, navy, or marine force. However, international events of the next 15 years would cause many Americans to reassess this position.

France and Great Britain continued to engage each other in a worldwide duel for foreign territory and, nearer home, a struggle for the domination of Europe. This confrontation resulted not only in warfare in continental Europe but also in sea warfare on most of the oceans of the world, especially in the Atlantic. Each side expected the United States to help it against the other. Britain had engaged the aid of the Muslim rulers of the North African coast—located in Algiers, Tunis, Tripoli, and Morocco (then called the Barbary States)—to harass merchant ships traveling in the Mediterranean Sea and the Atlantic Ocean. As a result of a treaty signed in 1793 between Britain and the Barbary States (as well as a sizable yearly payment on the part of Great Britain), British merchant ships were immune from attack by the Barbary privateers. However, the ships of other nations—including those of the United States—were not protected, and many were seized and held for ransom. In September 1795 the United States was forced to conclude a humiliating treaty with the Barbary States that stipulated payment of $1 million in return for limited protection for U.S. ships and sailors.

At about this time France began attacking and seizing American merchant ships as well. The French, led by an arrogant revolutionary government that demanded the United States side with France in its struggle against Great Britain, were angered by American neutrality. When the French government did not receive help from the United States, it ordered its ships to attack American merchant vessels. During the 18 months between July 1796 and January 1798 the French seized 316 American merchant ships.

Reluctantly, many Americans began to consider rebuilding the armed forces. Congress appropriated money for the construction of new ships, and by 1797 three vessels had been launched: the *United States*, the *Constitution*, and the *Constellation*. On July 11, 1798, Congress passed an act that provided for "establishing and organizing a Marine Corps," and the organization we know as the United States Marine Corps was officially born. The U.S. Senate was granted the authority to appoint all officers, and enlistment was set for three-year terms. Organizationally, the Marine Corps was to be a branch of the Department of the Navy (which had been created in April of that year). The commandant of the Marine Corps was appointed by the secretary of the navy, who at that time reported to the secretary of war.

The marines who enlisted in 1798 assumed the same tasks that their predecessors had shouldered during the revolutionary war. They kept discipline aboard ship, prepared for landings to attack enemy coastal settlements, and were expected to storm enemy warships during battles on the high seas. A fourth duty was added to these tasks: that of maintaining and defending

In 1798 President John Adams appointed Major William Ward Burrows of Philadelphia as the first commandant of the U.S. Marine Corps. During Burrows's tenure the Marine Band was formed, the marines' barracks were built in the nation's new capital, Washington, D.C., and the United States entered into war with the Barbary States.

fortifications on the Atlantic coast of the United States. An unfortunate provision of the 1798 bill that created the Marine Corps stipulated that Negroes, mulattoes (persons born to one white and one black parent), and Indians were barred from the corps. These groups were restricted from serving in the army and the navy as well, but after 1862 they were allowed to serve as soldiers and sailors in segregated units. (Racial integration of the armed forces did not occur until 1948, when President Harry S. Truman issued an executive order barring segregation in the military.)

On July 12, 1798, President John Adams appointed William Ward Burrows of Philadelphia as the first commandant of the U.S. Marine Corps. A detachment of marines, dressed in new blue uniforms with red piping, was mustered out in Philadelphia to serve on the USS *Constitution*. From the beginning there was friction between the navy and the Marine Corps. As members of a smaller organization within the larger navy, marines sometimes chafed under naval

35

Marine lieutenant Presley O'Bannon leads his troops over the walls of the fortress of Derna, Tripoli, in 1805. O'Bannon and his men captured the fortress, and their victory has been commemorated in the "Marines' Hymn" in the words *to the shores of Tripoli.*

authority. By the rules of the navy the captain of any ship was the overall commander of all people on board. Thus the marines—and their commander on the ship—were subordinate to the final authority of the ship's captain, a navy man. Nevertheless, Commandant Burrows expected his men to stand up for the corps, and the marines soon gained a growing reputation for esprit de corps and cockiness.

One of the first important assignments given the new U.S. Marine Corps was to take action against the bey of Tripoli, the leader of one of the Barbary States whose navy had attacked American merchant ships. In 1803 a squadron was sent into the Mediterranean to show the American flag and blockade

Tripoli. Bad luck struck the expedition almost at once. One of the squadron's ships, the *Philadelphia*, foundered on a reef, and 308 sailors—including 48 marines—were captured by the forces of the bey and held hostage for ransom.

The United States was not able to launch an effective counterstrike until 1805. A force led by marine lieutenant Presley O'Bannon and William Eaton, the newly appointed navy agent for the Barbary States and a former American diplomat to Tunis, was able to march from the Nile River in Egypt 600 miles across the desert to Derna, an important fortified town that guarded the route to Tripoli. Despite dissension and revolts among his largely Arab and Greek mercenary force, O'Bannon was able to defeat the bey's army in an attack coordinated with the U.S. ships *Argus*, *Hornet*, and *Nautilus* on April 27, 1805. This great victory was accompanied by a letdown when the USS *Constitution* arrived in Derna the day after the battle with the news that a treaty had been reached with the bey to ransom the prisoners taken from the *Philadelphia*. Although the United States had given in to the demands of the bey, the marines had no reason to be ashamed of their performance in North Africa. Presley O'Bannon returned to the United States as a hero, carrying the jeweled sword of the bey's exiled brother, his chief Arab ally.

War with Mexico

For the next 40 years the marines saw action mostly in the continental United States, first against the British in Washington, D.C., and New Orleans in the War of 1812 and later against the Seminole, Cherokee, Creek, and Chickasaw tribes in Georgia, Florida, and Alabama. Fought between 1836 and 1842, these Indian wars were sparked by the settlers' increasing demands for more land. It was during this time that the inhabitants of the eastern United States began their relentless push westward. The marines' next major battles resulted from this expansion and occurred during the war between the United States and Mexico that broke out in 1846.

For its part, Mexico had never recognized the independent Republic of Texas, which had been established in 1836 when the Texans defeated a military force led by Mexican general Antonio López de Santa Anna. So when, nearly a decade later, the citizens of Texas voted to join the United States, Mexican authorities strongly protested. The situation escalated into war after Mexican and American troops clashed in south Texas over a border dispute.

The marines' first engagements against Mexico took place in California, which was then still Mexican territory—land the United States hoped to

In 1847 marines under the command of Lieutenant Colonel Samuel Watson attack Chapultepec Hill at the entrance to Mexico City. The marines engaged in hand-to-hand combat with the Mexican forces, captured the palace at the top of the hill, and enabled army commander General Winfield Scott and the American forces to take Mexico City.

possess. Led by Lieutenant Archibald Gillespie and Captain Ward Marston, the marines, with the aid of American settlers, took the towns of Monterey and Yerba Buena (later known as San Francisco) in northern California. After a prolonged and difficult fight against Mexican forces, they routed the garrisons at San Diego and Los Angeles as well. The marines' toughest action during the war occurred in Mexico proper, however. There, 366 marines under the command of Lieutenant Colonel Samuel Watson were assigned the task of capturing Chapultepec Hill, a 200-foot-high knoll that commanded the entrance to Mexico City. The capture of Chapultepec was essential to the success of the larger 14,000-man American army force under the command of General Winfield Scott.

The marines made their assault on Chapultepec on September 13, 1847, in an attack that started at eight in the morning. The marine force split into two groups, one going up the west side of the slope and the other up the south side. Both groups engaged in fierce hand-to-hand fighting with bayonets and rifles, which they used as clubs. After an hour and a half both groups had reached the Chapultepec palace atop the hill, and by 9:30 the Stars and Stripes was fluttering from the hilltop, a signal to General Scott that he could send his larger force along the base of the hill toward Mexico City.

Once Chapultepec had been secured by U.S. forces, Watson's marines rushed to aid the army in its final push into Mexico City. By nightfall, they had taken the last two gates to the city. There they paused, planning to finish the attack in the morning. That night, however, the Mexican general Santa Anna withdrew what remained of his army, and at dawn the marines rushed to the National Palace at the center of the city, only to find it deserted. Because of their reputation for bravery, the marines were given the honor of guarding the National Palace for the duration of the American occupation of Mexico City. The palace, which was located on the site where the Aztec emperor Montezuma had once ruled, lent itself to a piece of marine history: The words *from the halls of Montezuma* begin the "Marines' Hymn," and, according to legend, the red stripes that run down the sides of marine dress trousers commemorate the blood of marines shed in the taking of Mexico City during the Mexican War.

Civil War

The next major challenge for the marines came during the epic struggle between the Northern and Southern states that was known as the Civil War. The Marine Corps received a shocking blow at the beginning of the war in April 1861 when a large number of its officers joined the Confederate forces of the South. Most of the enlisted marines, however, remained loyal to the corps and the Union.

The Civil War spurred enormous changes in the way the navy fought sea battles. Steam-powered engines replaced sail-driven vessels; newly invented high-explosive shells could destroy the wooden hulls of ships, thus prompting a changeover to steel-hulled boats; and rifled grooves were etched inside the barrels of ship guns to give them greater accuracy and firing distance.

Even though hundreds of thousands of men served in the Union army, the strength of the corps during the entire war never exceeded 3,900 men. This was in part because the corps still had a very limited mission at this time. It was also because its mission was in many ways no longer applicable, for the marines' role did not change as rapidly as did naval technology. The marines were used primarily to help enforce the blockade of Southern ports and were a sideshow to the main fighting, which was shouldered by the army.

The corps was burdened with an aging leadership, which also contributed to its small role in the fighting. Its commandant for most of the conflict (until May

1864) was John Harris, a veteran of the Mexican War. Harris had served in the Marine Corps for 44 years and was 70 years old by the time the Civil War began. He had neither the energy nor the vision to forge a strong and innovative role for the corps during this crucial period of its history.

Two events that occurred during the Civil War were indicative of the challenges facing the Marine Corps at this time. The first was the creation in the fall of 1861 of a special marine amphibious battalion—that is, a battalion whose specialty was seaborne assaults on coastal fortifications. Even though this group never made a combat landing during the war, it signaled a change in emphasis for the Marine Corps from a force that primarily fought on the open seas to one that increasingly would be landed from sea to fight on land.

The second significant event involved the duel between the ironclad ships the *Monitor* (a Union ship) and the *Virginia* (formerly the U.S. Navy vessel *Merrimack*, which had been scuttled by the Union and reclaimed by the Confederacy). The confrontation between the two ships began on the morning of March 8, 1862, when the *Virginia* steamed out of Hampton Roads, Virginia, to attack five wooden-hulled, sail-driven warships of the U.S. Navy. The Union vessels were stationed at the entrance of the James River to intercept ships coming and going from the Confederate port. The *Virginia* attacked the Union vessel *Cumberland* first. The initial shot from the strange-looking Confederate

Colonel John Harris, commandant of the Marine Corps from 1850 to 1864 and a veteran of the Mexican War, led the corps through most of the Civil War. Harris was nearly 70 years old when the Civil War began and had neither the strength nor the imagination to push the corps into taking an aggressive role in the conflict.

40

The Confederacy's ironclad ship Virginia *sinks the Union's ship* Cumberland *in 1862. Before the* Cumberland *was destroyed, the marines fired rifles and cannons at the* Virginia, *but the shots bounced off the iron-sheathed hull. Fourteen of the 46 marines on board the Union vessel were killed.*

boat—one of the first of its kind—killed several marines who had been standing in formation on the foredeck of the Union ship. Other marines from the *Cumberland* tried to shoot through the gun holes of the Confederate vessel, but both rifle fire and cannon shots bounced off the *Virginia*'s iron-sheathed turret and hull. Meanwhile, the *Virginia* kept up a steady fire against the *Cumberland* and eventually sank the ship, killing 14 of the 46 marines on board. The battle continued for the rest of the day until finally the *Virginia* withdrew to port. During the course of the battle the Confederate ship sank two Union ships and caused the grounding of one other. It had been a spectacular day for the Confederacy and a dismal one for both the Union and the marines. The next day the *Virginia* ventured out into the bay once again only to be confronted with its twin, the ironclad Union ship *Monitor.* The two vessels engaged in an intense close-range gunfight for four hours, and the battle finally ended when the *Virginia* scored a direct hit on the *Monitor*'s pilot house. This was the first face-to-face battle between iron-hulled, steam-driven warships, and it heralded the advent of new technology that would change the nature of sea warfare. The marines' place in this new order was uncertain. What did seem sure was that their days of storming enemy ships on the high seas were over.

*President Theodore Roosevelt conducts a quartet of American advisers in
Panama in this 1906 cartoon lampooning the tactics the U.S. government
used to achieve its goal of building a canal across the Isthmus of Panama. In
a speech made early in his presidency, Roosevelt had quoted the old adage
Speak softly and carry a big stick in reference to executing American foreign
policy abroad. Frequently, the "big stick" he used was the U.S. Marine Corps.*

THREE

The Big Stick

Following the Civil War, the Marine Corps once again entered a period of stagnation. More than 500,000 soldiers and civilians from the North and the South had been killed or wounded during the conflict. Americans were tired of warfare, and they were in no mood to turn their energies to defense matters. Even though the army would fight a 20-year battle with various American Indian tribes in the West, the United States would not be at war with a European nation for another 33 years. Many citizens simply lost interest in the readiness of the armed forces during this period, and as a result all branches of the U.S. military—including the Marine Corps—were neglected.

If there was any single, great theme of this era in the United States it was economic expansion. The end of the 19th century was a time of national renewal and intense economic activity. The U.S. economy grew steadily, spurring new waves of immigration to America. The industrial cities of the North grew rapidly. Drawn by the allure of cheap land, pioneers continued to flock to the western frontiers. American merchant traders pushed southward into Latin America and eastward to Asia, opening up new spheres of trade for U.S. goods. This was by and large a hopeful time, and with the exception of the Indian wars, it was a time of peace and prosperity.

Because the Marine Corps had no role in the Indian conflict, it could not demand money for new recruits, new training, or new equipment. As a result,

Charles McCawley served as commandant of the Marine Corps from 1876 to 1891. The son of a marine captain, McCawley focused his efforts on raising the standards for enlistment, developing a more highly trained force, and improving the selection and instruction of officers.

its influence within the armed forces shrank. Jacob Zeilin, a veteran of the Civil War, was commandant of the corps from 1864 to 1876. During his tenure the number of men in the corps dropped to as low as 2,000—roughly the strength of the marines during the revolutionary war more than 80 years earlier. At one point in 1866, membership in the corps had decreased so much that the House of Representatives directed its Committee on Naval Affairs to consider abolishing the force. The committee held hearings, listened to witnesses, and concluded, "No good reason appears either for abolishing the Marine Corps or transferring it to the Army; on the contrary the Committee recommends that its organization as a separate Corps be preserved."

When Zeilin retired in 1876, another hero of the Civil War, Charles McCawley, was chosen to replace him. McCawley, who served as commandant until 1891, was remembered chiefly as the man who hired John Philip Sousa as the director of the Marine Band. Sousa stayed with the band for 12 years, during which time he wrote more than 100 of the marches that made him famous. It was during his tenure that the "Marines' Hymn" became popular. The origin of this song is obscure: Marine tradition ascribes the composition of the lyrics to an unknown marine during the time of the occupation of Mexico City in 1847. It is believed that the marine then set his words to the music of the "Gendarme's Song" in the opera *Genevieve de Brabant* by the French composer Jacques Offenbach. However it came into being, the "Marines' Hymn" has remained a well-known and well-loved song and is the tune most clearly associated with the United States Marine Corps.

McCawley's other legacy was to upgrade the quality of the marine officer corps by insisting that as many officers as possible attend and graduate from the U.S. Naval Academy in Annapolis, Maryland. Between 1883 and 1897 all of the new officers of the corps—and there were only 50 during this period—were graduates of the U.S. Naval Academy. Graduation from the academy had long been one route to joining the corps as an officer. A great many marine officers before the 1880s were not graduates of the academy, however. A commission to officer status could be gained directly by appoint-

John Philip Sousa (center) directed the Marine Band from 1880 to 1892. During his tenure, Sousa wrote more than 100 of the marches that made him the March King, including "The Thunderer," "Semper Fidelis," and "Washington Post."

Commandant Charles Heywood led the Marine Corps from 1891 to 1903. Heywood was successful in obtaining funds from Congress and the War Department to modernize the corps's weaponry with such innovations as the multibarreled Gatling gun.

ment of the U.S. Senate, and occasionally enlisted men worked their way into the officer ranks through dedication and long service to the corps. University training was not seen as necessary or particularly important for the early marine officers: Bravery and fighting spirit were not characteristics that could be taught in a classroom. But with the increasing prominence of new technologies in warfare in the late 1800s, an officer with an engineering or science degree from the academy became a valuable commodity for the Marine Corps, and a college-educated officer found his chances for promotion within the corps considerably enhanced.

The Marine Corps finally managed to catch up with the changing times and technology in the 1890s, when Colonel Charles Heywood assumed command. Heywood instituted a series of training courses for officers and made promotion procedures more regular and impartial. He also managed to get money from Congress and the War Department to modernize the corps's weaponry. The marines finally gave up their old breech-loading muskets and adopted the new .45 caliber Springfield rifle, which could be loaded and fired more rapidly. The corps also managed to obtain the new multibarreled Gatling gun, the precursor of the machine gun, which was one of the new weapons whose use so dramatically changed the nature of warfare during World War I (1914–18). Finally, the strength of the Marine Corps increased during Heywood's tenure: from 75 officers and 2,100 enlisted men in 1891 to 278 officers and 7,532 enlisted men in 1903, when he retired.

The Monroe Doctrine, Latin America, and the Marines

As America grew economically during the latter half of the 19th century, its citizens and leaders began to rethink earlier ideas of the nation's place in the world. Ideas such as self-sufficiency and the notion that one nation should not interfere in the internal affairs of another—popular in earlier, revolutionary America—were now jettisoned. With its union strongly reaffirmed following the Civil War and its economy booming, the United States now saw itself on equal footing with the world powers of the time. If other nations could pursue their economic self-interests to the four corners of the earth, then the United States could as well.

The European powers—Great Britain, France, and Spain—were unapologetic colonialists: That is, they believed that the direct political subjugation and control of other peoples and countries of the world were not only right but also necessary for the interests of the imperial mother nation. As a result, by the late 19th century Britain controlled a worldwide empire that included a number of islands in the Caribbean, large parts of Africa, all of the subcontinent of India, the Malay Peninsula, Australia, and Canada. France controlled other large areas of Africa, some Caribbean islands, and most of Indochina. Spain, whose empire had once consisted of virtually all of Latin America (except Brazil), was now reduced to ownership of Cuba, Puerto Rico, and the Philippines. (Even tiny Holland maintained a colony, the Netherlands East Indies, among the islands of the Malay Archipelago.)

These were the countries with which the United States saw itself in competition. To equal or better these nations in the realm of international power politics, American leaders felt obliged to play the game of world colonialism, too, but with a slightly different twist. Because the United States itself was a former colony, strong residual feelings against colonialism still existed among many of its citizens. Thus, the American government could not follow the European model step-for-step. The United States could not nakedly proclaim itself an imperial power and begin grabbing less developed parts of the world for itself. More noble and enlightened reasons for territorial expansion had to be constructed. One of the most useful justifications for American interference in the affairs of other nations—at least other nations in the Western Hemisphere—was found in a proclamation made in 1823 by President James Monroe. Known as the Monroe Doctrine, this statement insisted that no new colonies could be established in the Western Hemisphere by European colonial powers.

Monroe issued his proclamation in reaction to what turned out to be a minor dispute with Russia over the U.S. government's claim to an area of the Pacific Northwest (which today comprises the states of Oregon and Washington). Monroe also feared that several European nations had plans to try to recolonize some of the newly independent Latin American nations, which had only recently succeeded in revolting against Spanish rule. The United States decided to assume the position of protector of these countries. This attitude was not welcomed by the Latin American nations, however, which conducted their own affairs without the "advice" of the United States.

In the end, Monroe's fears about Russia and European recolonization of the Americas were unfounded. A treaty was worked out with the Russian government in 1825 recognizing the United States's right to the Pacific Northwest. And for many years no European power was able to mount any serious threat to the independent Latin American republics. Nonetheless, after the Civil War the United States began invoking the Monroe Doctrine as its

Marines aboard the battleship California, *en route to Nicaragua in 1912. The Monroe Doctrine (1823), which insisted that no new colonies could be established in the Western Hemisphere by European powers, was frequently invoked by the United States as justification for its interference in the affairs of Latin America. The federal government sent the Marine Corps into the region to safeguard U.S. interests.*

excuse to send its own armed forces—usually the marines—into the Latin American republics.

The first interventions actually occurred just before the Civil War. The United States dispatched the marines to Nicaragua on several occasions in the 1850s, giving as its reason its "right" under the Monroe Doctrine to safeguard its interests in the Western Hemisphere. The particular interest was a highly profitable ferry line that was owned and operated by the American industrialist Cornelius Vanderbilt. The line, which linked the Pacific Ocean to the Caribbean Sea, became an issue in Nicaraguan politics when the Conservative party, which supported Vanderbilt, became embroiled in a civil war with the Liberal party. The Liberals wanted to confiscate the business and put it in the hands of Nicaraguan owners. In addition, soldiers loyal to the Liberal party had briefly seized the U.S. ambassador. To counter this threat to American lives and property, the United States sent in the marines.

Other expeditions to Latin America followed the marines' first landings in Nicaragua. Marines were shipped to Panama in 1873 and 1885 to guard a railroad project that the national government of Colombia threatened to confiscate. (At that time Panama was not an independent country, but a province of Colombia.) American investors had spent millions of dollars constructing a railroad across the Isthmus of Panama that would haul goods back and forth between the Caribbean Sea and the Pacific Ocean. This railroad would considerably shorten the amount of time needed to ship goods and troops from the Atlantic to the Pacific coasts and thus was considered important to American national interests.

The irony of the United States's actions in Nicaragua and Panama—and in later interventions in Asia and other parts of Latin America—was that the U.S. government behaved in a way that would have been intolerable to American citizens had another nation tried to intervene in U.S. affairs in a similar manner. That is, no American would have permitted Great Britain or France to send troops into the United States to "protect" its investments on American soil. British and French investments were welcomed, but they were subject to U.S. law. The U.S. government had the right to tax them at a high rate—or even to insist that Americans own a certain share of the investments. The federal government could even vote to confiscate these investments. These decisions were made by Americans themselves, not by a foreign government. But this was not how the United States chose to treat weaker and poorer nations in Latin America, and most often the instrument the government used to enforce this undemocratic rule by force was the United States Marine Corps.

The leadership of the marines could not and did not protest the role the corps was called on to play in Latin America. The Marine Corps was at the command of a civilian, democratically elected government, and neither the marine commandant nor any other officers made the crucial decisions about whether or not to intervene in the affairs of other nations. This decision could be made only by the president. However, once ordered into action the marines responded enthusiastically. They had their reputation as an elite fighting unit to uphold, and in this they succeeded magnificently.

The incursions into Nicaragua and Panama were brief and did not really put the Marine Corps to the test. By far the most important challenge to the corps during this era came in 1898 with the outbreak of war between the United States and Spain. For some time tensions had been mounting between the two countries over the independence of Cuba. Many Cubans, including the famous leader José Martí, had for years worked for Cuban independence while residing in the United States, and the sympathy of the American public was on the side of the Cuban rebels.

On February 15, 1898, the USS *Maine*, an American navy cruiser, was blown up in Havana's harbor, killing 28 marines and 222 sailors. Even though the cause of the explosion was never discovered, the American press blamed the Spanish and called for war to avenge the death of the crew. Both the press and the government knew that once-powerful Spain was now an enfeebled giant; its days of empire and glory were in the past. It had become one of the poorest countries in western Europe, and its military strength was uncertain.

In spite of Spain's dwindling power, no one was prepared for the swiftness of the American victory. Congress declared war against Spain on April 25, 1898. On April 30, Commodore George Dewey's flotilla, sailing from Hong Kong, surprised and destroyed the Spanish fleet in Manila Bay in the Philippines.

The Marine Corps's most important role in the war was to secure the port of Guantánamo Bay, Cuba. On June 10 the first marine detachment landed in

In 1898, during the Spanish-American War, marines pose for a picture at their camp at Guantánamo, Cuba. The Marine Corps made an amphibious landing at the port of Guantánamo in June 1898 and established a stronghold there. (Guantánamo continues to serve as a U.S. naval base today.) Four months later, the United States defeated Spain.

51

Guantánamo with little opposition. The First Marine Battalion set up head-quarters under the palms on the east side of the bay. Their first encounter with the Spanish came the next day, when two marines were killed by a Spanish ambush. Sporadic guerrilla fighting continued for the next several days, until the battalion was ordered to destroy a well six miles away that was the source of water for the Spanish camp. On June 14 the marines marched to the site of the well and, supported by gunfire from the American cruiser *Dolphin*, routed the Spanish defenders. Tactics to sight naval gunfire were still somewhat primitive in 1898, and at one point during the engagement shells from the ship began falling near the marines. Sergeant John Quick, a native of West Virginia, rigged a signal flag with a handkerchief and stick to redirect the artillery fire. By doing this, Quick exposed himself to Spanish fire. He was successful in his mission, however, and was not wounded. As a result of his bravery he was awarded the Medal of Honor, the highest U.S. military honor for bravery in action.

By early August the marines and the army had routed the Spanish. On August 12, less than four months after the Spanish-American War began, the United States and Spain agreed to end the fighting.

The Spanish-American War was important for the marines in two ways. First, it proved their continued usefulness in defending foreign bases for the navy in times of war. Guantánamo was vital to the American war effort in Cuba because it served as a stepping-off point for inland campaigns. Furthermore, it was one of the U.S. military's most important strategic bases during the first part of the 20th century.

The Spanish-American War was also important because now marines increasingly would be used to enforce American foreign policy in the Caribbean region of Latin America. In Cuba, for instance, marines were stationed on garrison duty in Havana between 1899 and 1902, between 1906 and 1909, in 1912, and from 1917 to 1922 to protect American business interests and help stabilize the volatile Cuban government. Frequently the Marine Corps was used as an armed force to back whichever Cuban political party promised the best deal to U.S. businesses. The Platt Amendment, which was written into the Cuban constitution in June 1901 at the insistence of the U.S. government, allowed the United States to intervene in Cuban affairs in order to preserve Cuban independence and protect human life and property.

In 1904, President Theodore Roosevelt proclaimed a corollary, or addition, to the Monroe Doctrine that explicitly claimed for the United States the right to intervene anywhere in the Western Hemisphere. This right, Roosevelt said,

A marine gun crew stationed in the Panama Canal Zone in 1913. From 1903, when the United States obtained the right to build a canal across Panama, to 1914, when the Panama Canal was opened, marines helped defend the Canal Zone and protected U.S. interests in the area.

was unilateral—that is, the U.S. government could make its decision on its own, without consulting any other nation.

Roosevelt had issued this statement to justify a military adventure he had masterminded just two years earlier. In 1903, with the backing of the U.S. government and American businesses, Panamanian rebels declared their province independent of Colombian rule. In response, the Colombians sent 4,000 soldiers to Colon, Panama, a port town on the Caribbean Sea, to put down the rebels. Marines under the command of Major John Lejeune were landed from the USS *Nashville* to stop the Colombian troops from attacking the rebels. They successfully accomplished this task without bloodshed, and the Panamanians achieved their independence.

This U.S.-backed independence movement was convenient for the United States because American businesses were scheming to continue work on the

In 1919 marines scour the Haitian countryside looking for bandits. The Marine Corps was sent to Haiti in 1915 to protect U.S. economic interests and remained there for 19 years.

transisthmus canal through Panama. The French had begun construction of the canal in 1881 but had abandoned the project several years later when it proved to be too costly. The canal, completed in 1914, was a major engineering triumph for the United States. It allowed ships to pass from the Atlantic to the Pacific oceans without having to make the 3,000-mile trip around Cape Horn at the tip of South America. In 1903 Panama and the United States had signed a treaty granting the U.S. government control of the strip of land on which the canal was to be built. According to the treaty the United States would maintain this right forever, but forever proved to be not quite as long as imagined. In the late 1970s the United States signed a new treaty, promising to turn control of the canal over to Panama by the year 2000.

During the early part of the 20th century the Marine Corps was also active in Nicaragua, Haiti, the Dominican Republic, and Mexico. In 1912 marines were sent to Nicaragua to guarantee the safety of American companies that carried out trade in the tropical lowlands of the Caribbean coast. They performed essentially the same role as they had during their earlier interventions there in the 1850s. As before, they helped the Conservative party in its struggle against the Liberals' efforts to seize power. And, as before, the United States backed the Conservatives because they offered American business interests better deals. The new government allowed 2 American banks to set up the Nicaraguan national bank and to run the customs service in order to recoup with interest a $14 million loan they had made to the previous government. By early 1913 most of the marines had been pulled out of Nicaragua, but they returned again in 1926 to guard American property when fighting again broke out between the Conservatives and Liberals. The marines soon became the target of a group of Liberal rebels led by Augusto C. Sandino, whose forces fled to the jungles of northern Nicaragua and carried on a guerrilla war with the marines until 1933, when American troops were removed from the country.

The marines were sent to Haiti in July 1915 for the same reason they had been sent to Nicaragua: to protect economic interests of American companies. This time the main American company demanding action was the National City Bank of New York, which stood to lose several hundred thousand dollars in gold bullion (uncoined gold in bar form) that it had loaned to the Haitian national bank. As in Nicaragua, internal political parties were locked in a power struggle. The previous Haitian president, Vilbrun Guillaume Sam, had been hacked to death by a mob in the Haitian capital of Port-au-Prince. No strong government stood ready to replace President Sam, and it was rumored that the national bank was going to be stormed and the gold reserves taken. After the marines landed on July 28 and restored order, they gradually assumed command of the Haitian national police. The marine commander, Colonel Tony Waller (and later Brigadier General Eli Cole), became the day-to-day ruler of the country, even though a president and parliament still existed.

The marines stayed in Haiti for 19 years. Throughout this occupation, they fought more or less constant guerrilla wars with Haitian resistance fighters known as the *cacos*, who took their name from a Haitian bird of prey. As it did with Cuba, the U.S. government signed a treaty with Haiti that made the American occupation of this foreign nation appear to have some legality and legitimacy. In fact, the people of Haiti always opposed the presence of the marines and applauded a U.S. commission's recommendations in 1930 to gradually withdraw the troops.

The marine excursions into Mexico in 1914 and the Dominican Republic from 1916 to 1924 were also carried out for economic reasons. Latin American nations came to resent this high-handed American approach to their region, and the prestige of the United States declined in the nations south of the border. American interference in Latin American affairs would not diminish until Franklin D. Roosevelt became president in 1933. Roosevelt instituted the Good Neighbor Policy, which—although it never promised that the United States would stay completely out of the affairs of Latin American nations—did pledge that his administration would be much more careful about intervention in these countries.

China and the Philippines

In its drive for influence and power throughout the world, the United States not only pushed southward into Latin America but also eastward into Asia. In this second area the marines again played a prominent role. The first major muscle flexing by the United States occurred in April 1854. Sixty sailors and marines from the sloop *Plymouth* were sent ashore at Shanghai, China, to defend the American trade settlement there from attack by insurgents fighting against the decadent Manchu dynasty (1644–1911). (The Manchu dynasty was also called the Qing dynasty, which was founded in China by conquerors from Manchuria.) On April 4 a combined force of American and British troops routed the Chinese from the foreign settlement. This contingent of U.S. Marines was in Asia as part of a larger group that had been sent to Japan by President Millard Fillmore to open up Japan to American trade goods. The leader of the expedition, Commodore Matthew Perry of the U.S. Navy, met with Japanese dignitaries in Yokohama in March 1854. Flanked by a marine honor guard, the parties signed the Treaty of Kanagawa, which opened two Japanese ports to U.S. trade.

The marines were sent to China again in 1856 to protect the American trade settlement in Canton, but they did not see much action in the country for the rest of the 19th century. This period of calm came to a dramatic end in 1900, when China became wracked by political upheaval. A group of rebels, officially called the Fists of Righteous Harmony but popularly known as the Boxers, sought to topple the weak Manchu regime that ruled from the capital of Peking. They wanted to replace the ancient dynasty with a stronger government that

56

would throw all foreigners out of China. The United States, Britain, France, Germany, and Russia had effectively carved China into separate zones of influence, and the Manchus had lost the power to govern in large parts of the country.

The Boxers attacked foreign embassies and trading posts throughout China, but their activity was most ferocious in the northern part of the country. They encircled and cut off Peking in June 1900, isolating it for 55 days. The more than 3,000 foreigners of various nationalities living in the Chinese capital were protected by a group of 56 marines and sailors and a few hundred soldiers from an assortment of countries. Marine captain John Myers led the combined troops.

The foreigners had gathered together in a section of Peking called the Legation Quarter, which was three-quarters of a mile square and protected in some places by handmade barricades and in others by high walls. Outside, bands of Boxers roved the city and tried to storm the barricades and walls of the Legation Quarter. In the meantime, a relief force of U.S. Marines and British and Russian soldiers gathered at the port of Tientsin in order to march on Peking. The First Marine Regiment, commanded by Major William Biddle, represented the marines. The trek across the Chinese plains was grueling in the heat of summer. The relief force was under constant attack by Boxers as they marched to Peking, but the force finally reached the outskirts of the city

A soldier mans a cannon inside Peking's Legation Quarter during the Boxer Rebellion in 1900. For nearly two months, Chinese rebels surrounded the Legation Quarter, which was defended by several hundred soldiers— including 56 U.S. Marines and sailors— from an assortment of countries.

on August 13. As the relief force approached the next day, the Boxers tried desperately to storm the Legation Quarter but were repulsed by the marines and the other forces inside the compound. In this fight a young marine private named Dan Daly led a charge that stopped an attack near the Tung Pien gate. For his courage, Daly was awarded his first Medal of Honor. (He won his second for action in Haiti in 1915.)

With the appearance of Biddle's added forces the rebellion was effectively quelled, and the siege of the city was lifted. Soon afterward, the marines were withdrawn from China. They returned briefly in 1911, when 500 marines arrived in Peking to guard the American compound during the fall of the Manchu dynasty. Five thousand marines—one-quarter of the entire corps— were sent to Shanghai in 1927, when fighting between General Chiang Kai-shek, one of the most powerful Chinese political and military leaders, and other warlords broke out. Shanghai was the most important industrial and trading city in China and many Western businesses were headquartered there. The marines stood by to protect the large trade settlement if needed. Even though they never saw any combat and most were pulled out of Shanghai after the crisis passed, a small detachment of marines remained, which was strengthened in times of trouble. Few marines were needed until 1937, when

A detachment of marines clashes with Philippine insurgents in the early 1900s. Philippine rebels fought U.S. military rule of the islands until 1901, when their leader, Emilio Aguinaldo, was captured and took an oath of allegiance to the United States. Soon afterward the United States established a civilian government there, which governed the colony until 1946.

Japanese troops invaded China and threatened Shanghai. More than 2,500 marines, known as the China marines, were dispatched to Shanghai to guard American lives and property and remained there until just before the United States entered World War II in December 1941. Most were finally evacuated to the Philippines on November 27, 1941, only 10 days before the Japanese attacked the American naval station at Pearl Harbor, Hawaii.

Marine involvement in the Philippines began in 1898, when Commodore Dewey destroyed the Spanish fleet in Manila Bay at the start of the Spanish-American War. The marines saw heavy action in the Philippines—not against the Spanish but against a group of rebels who fought for Philippine independence. After the battle of Manila Bay, Emilio Aguinaldo, a Filipino revolutionary who had been exiled to Hong Kong by the Spanish several years earlier, was brought back to the Philippines by the U.S. fleet. When it became apparent after the war that the Americans were not planning to leave the islands, Aguinaldo and his followers rose in rebellion and declared an independent republic. They melted into the jungles and mountains to fight a guerrilla war against the marines. The struggle lasted until 1901, when Aguinaldo was captured and he declared an oath of allegiance to the United States. That same year, American military government of the islands ended and was replaced by a system run by a U.S.-appointed civilian governor. William Howard Taft, who would later become president of the United States, was appointed the first governor in 1901. The Philippines would remain a colony of the United States until 1946, and the marines would be stationed there, at their base at Cavite, until the very end.

The period from the last days of the Civil War to roughly the beginning of World War I was one of growing worldwide activity on the part of the marines. It was also marked by political decisions made in Washington that thrust the corps into situations where its presence was not always welcomed or appreciated. For better or worse, during this era the marines assumed the reputation, at least in Latin America, as America's "big stick," the military organization that was frequently called on to ensure that U.S. foreign policy was carried out. The corps had grown in both firepower and manpower. In 1916 more men than ever—13,600—proudly called themselves marines. The Marine Corps had grown beyond its traditional role as a naval fighting force. Now it had the size to stake out a role as a full-blown expeditionary force of the U.S. military. And now, if the American government needed to station an armed contingent permanently or semipermanently overseas, it would more than likely call on the marines. This was a role that the corps cherished and would not easily give up.

Five marines and one sailor raise the American flag atop Mount Suribachi, Iwo Jima, on February 23, 1945. This Pulitzer Prize–winning photograph by Associated Press photographer Joe Rosenthal served as the model for the Marine Corps Memorial at Arlington National Cemetery in Virginia.

FOUR

An American Century

Eighteen years after it lifted the siege of Peking in 1900, the United States Marine Corps entered a new phase of its history. Like the other branches of the U.S. armed forces it was called on by the American government to help break the military deadlock between Germany and the Allied governments of Britain, France, and Russia during World War I. By 1917, when the first small force of American servicemen landed in Europe, both Germany and the Allies were exhausted from three long years of war. Nearly 7 million soldiers had been killed by then, and 18 to 19 million more had been wounded. Both sides had used up their will to fight, yet neither wanted to be the first to ask for peace after having made such terrible sacrifices.

President Woodrow Wilson had campaigned for reelection in 1916 on the promise of keeping the United States out of the war, but German submarine attacks on American ships and Allied pressure to join the war effort pushed the United States into the conflict. On April 6, 1917—only four months after his reelection—President Wilson signed a declaration of war against Germany.

Marines gather around a German trench mortar captured during the battle of Belleau Wood, a fierce confrontation waged 40 miles northeast of Paris in June 1918. The Germans were so impressed by the extraordinary fighting skills and determination of the marines that they nicknamed them Teufel- hunden, or Devil Dogs, an epithet the marines still bear with pride.

World War I

It took the U.S. military a full year to gear up for the war. The first large contingents of U.S. soldiers were not in place in France to help the Allied war effort until the spring of 1918. It was at this moment that Germany, sensing that time was running out for a victory, launched its last, desperate offensives against the Allies. One of the most important of these campaigns was an effort to break through the Allied lines and take Paris. On May 27, 1918, the Germans launched an offensive near the town of Château-Thierry, only 40 miles northeast of Paris. The attackers quickly took the town and from there proceeded toward Paris through a place called Bois de Belleau, known in English as the Belleau Wood. It was here that the Germans encountered for the first time the men of the U.S. Marine Corps's Fourth Brigade.

The Fourth Brigade, known simply as the Marine Brigade, was a unit of 8,211 enlisted men and 258 officers. It was attached to the Second Division of the American Expeditionary Force (the name of the American forces in Europe). The overall commander of these troops was army general John Pershing. At Belleau Wood the corps was fighting far from the ocean. This was a new role for the marines, a role that had resulted from the farsightedness of some of the corps's top officers.

In 1915 the quick-thinking assistant to the commandant, Colonel John Lejeune, gained approval for a shift in the Marine Corps's traditional assignment. Anticipating that the United States would enter the war in Europe, Lejeune acknowledged that the marines' role against naval powers was to defend U.S. naval bases in foreign territory. However, against nonnaval powers, Lejeune declared that the marines should be "the Advance Guard of the Army . . . first to set foot on hostile soil in order to seize, fortify, or to hold a port from which as a base, the Army would prosecute its campaign." By 1918 Lejeune and Commandant George Barnett had pushed this concept even further, winning for the corps the position of vanguard soldiers who would fight wherever they were needed, even away from ports of embarkation, in the event of war in Europe. The army was reluctant to allow the Marine Corps into what it felt was its territory of fighting, but when General Pershing sailed for Europe with the first group of American troops on June 14, 1917, he took with him 2,759 men of the Fourth Marine Brigade. They constituted one-fifth of Pershing's original force.

The marines were sent to Belleau Wood to fill in the gaps of the tattered and demoralized French army. The area they were given to defend was north of the main highway to Paris. To the south the French had placed the Second Division of the U.S. Army. Both the army and the marines were stretched thin in defending this piece of French territory. Even though thousands of American soldiers had begun to pour into the ports of France, the Allied forces still lacked enough men to defend the whole line. By chance the Germans decided to direct their attack to the north of the highway through the marine sector. Had they gone even two or three miles to one side or the other, the Germans might have been able to sweep past the Americans. As it was, the marines had to fight for their life.

The French officer in charge commanded the marines to dig trenches from which to fight and to hold their line at any cost. This order was immediately countermanded by the marine commander, Brigadier General James G. Harbord. "The marines will hold where they stand," he said, but they would not dig in. Instead they prepared for a mobile response to a frontal attack.

The Germans came storming out of the woods on the afternoon of June 3, 1918. They had already routed the French army in Château-Thierry and were at the peak of their strength in the offensive. The marines held their fire until the Germans were only 100 yards away, then hit them hard as they crossed a wheat field in front of the woods. After several hours of intense fighting the men of the Fourth Brigade had stopped the Germans and sent them retreating back into the woods. Soon after this attack, an exhausted French officer stumbled into the marine ranks and demanded that they retreat. The reply of Captain Lloyd Williams has gone down in marine history. "Retreat, hell," Williams said. "We just got here."

For two days the marines and the Germans were locked in a standoff. Finally, on June 6 the marines received orders to go into the woods and push the Germans out. At first they marched bravely in neat lines from the wheat field into the woods. The Germans had placed machine gun pits strategically so that if one was taken it could be fired upon by yet another hidden farther in the woods. Snipers also shot at the marines from the tops of trees. The marines were exposed by their disciplined lines, and many men were killed in the first hours of battle. Finally the marines broke their lines and began fighting in small groups from clearing to clearing. At about 5:00 P.M., before the start of the second phase of their offensive, one group of marines rested as they regrouped for attack. This unit, the Seventy-third Machine Gun Company of the Third Battalion, had lost its commanding officer and now was led by a grizzled veteran of Peking and Haiti, the two-time Medal of Honor winner, First Sergeant Dan Daly. A correspondent from the Chicago *Tribune* described what happened next:

> An old gunnery sergeant commanded the platoon in the absence of the lieutenant, who had been shot and was out of sight. This old sergeant was a Marine veteran. His cheeks were bronzed with the wind and sun of the seven seas. The service bar across his left breast showed that he had fought in the Philippines, in Santo Domingo, at the walls of Peking, and in the streets of Vera Cruz. . . .
>
> As the minute for the advance arrived, he arose from the trees first and jumped out onto the exposed edge of the field that ran with lead, across which he and his men were to charge. Then he turned to give the charge order to the men of his platoon—his mates—the men he loved. He said: 'Come on, you sons-o'-bitches! Do you want to live forever?'

The fight went on through the evening and into the night. By morning the marines had a foothold in Belleau Wood, and another group had penetrated German positions to the south. Thirty-one officers and 1,056 enlisted men

Dan Daly, a scrappy ex-boxer from New York City, was twice awarded the Medal of Honor for bravery in action—once for his heroic feats in Peking and a second time for his valiant acts in Haiti. When the commanding officer of his company was shot at Belleau Wood in June 1918, the 45-year-old Daly took over, rallying his men to charge the Germans and earning a third commendation for the Medal of Honor.

were wounded or killed that day. The fighting went on for another two weeks before the marines finally pushed the Germans out of Belleau Wood.

The Germans had thrown everything they had at the marines, and the marines not only held their position, they emerged victorious. In gratitude, the French parliament declared July 4 a national holiday. The French commander of the sector where the marines fought ordered that Belleau Wood be renamed Bois de la Brigade de Marine. All American units sent small groups to Paris for a parade held in their honor on the Fourth of July. French premier Georges Clemenceau offered to open the brothels of Paris to the Americans, but General Pershing declined this gesture of appreciation. Perhaps the greatest honor granted the marines was the new nickname they had acquired from their German adversaries: Teufelhunden (Devil Dogs).

Marines parade through the streets of Paris after the battle of Belleau Wood, which thwarted the German advance on Paris. The French parliament expressed its appreciation to the U.S. troops by declaring the Fourth of July a national holiday and holding a parade in the Americans' honor.

This victory in a small area of rural France marked the beginning of the end for Germany. Running out of reinforcements and meeting continually replenished American forces, the German front began to buckle. A second German attack was defeated in Soissons in mid-July, and the German troops were forced back 10 miles from their original positions. Throughout October 1918 American and French forces pressed their attacks, and slowly the German army was pushed back. When a revolt broke out among civilians in Germany, the German government decided the time had come to seek peace. A general armistice with the Allied forces was signed on November 11. Germany had given in; the war was over.

The Interlude

World War I caused a need for more manpower and new thinking in the Marine Corps that resulted in several significant innovations. The number of marines jumped from 13,700 officers and enlisted men in 1917 to 75,000 by the end of the war. For the first time a Marine Corps Reserve was created, composed of more than 7,000 marines who held mostly administrative jobs in the corps throughout the United States. Through the Marine Reserves women were allowed to join the corps for the first time. World War I was also the first conflict in which the Marine Corps used airplanes in combat.

The corps was lucky that in the years immediately following the war it had one of its most energetic and imaginative leaders as commandant. Major General John Lejeune, the architect of the advance-guard concept that had put the marines in the center of action in France, assumed command of the corps in 1920. Lejeune was concerned that, despite the splendid reputation the Marine Corps had earned in World War I, it still did not have a clear and distinct strategy that would set it apart from the army and the navy. The very success of the corps in World War I had created jealousy and tension between the corps

Women marines are sworn in to the Marine Corps Reserve on August 17, 1918. Women were allowed to join the armed forces for the first time during World War I; almost 300 women served in the Marine Corps during the war.

Women in the Marines

There is a story in marine folklore that claims that the first woman marine was Lucy Brewer, who disguised herself as a man and served aboard the USS *Constitution* during the War of 1812. It is, however, impossible to verify this tale. The first woman, officially documented, to serve in the Marine Corps is listed in the marine archives in Washington, D.C. She was Opha Johnson, a civilian clerk at Marine Corps headquarters, and she enrolled in the Marine Corps Reserve on August 13, 1918.

America's involvement in World War I put great strains on both civilian and military work forces in the United States and enabled women to enter many areas of employment that had previously been denied them. The secretary of the navy at the time, Josephus Daniels, was a man of liberal imagination who welcomed women into the navy and the Marine Corps as a way of dealing with the increased wartime need for personnel. In March 1917 he put out a "Call to Colors" to the women of the United States to join the ranks of the navy. In spite of the resistance of most naval officers, Daniels was able to enlist women in the navy because naval regulations referred to the enlistment of "persons" (unlike the army, which specified "male persons"). By July 1918 the marines were ready to follow suit.

Thousands of women responded to the Marine Corps's offer. Women were enlisted in New York, Indianapolis, Denver, San Francisco, and dozens of other cities across America. In New York City alone hundreds lined up at the 23rd Street recruitment office in response to a newspaper article soliciting "intelligent young women." The process for joining was rigorous. In addition to being asked about their family and work experience, applicants were required to take a shorthand and stenographic test administered at breakneck speed. Those who passed worked mostly as typists and clerks in marine recruitment offices, quartermasters' and paymasters' offices (which were responsible for such matters as food, clothing, equipment, and wages), and at marine headquarters in Washington. By joining the corps, women freed thousands of male marines for overseas duty. (The time had not yet come when the marines would allow women to serve overseas.) All of the women were enrolled in the enlisted ranks. Female privates received the same pay as males: $15 a month plus an additional $83 for food and quarters.

For the most part the male marines were not thrilled by their new comrades in arms. The women were given such epithets as the Lady Hell Cats and the Skirt Marines, but after a time the men learned to respect the skill and dedication of the women. Like most of the men, the women were required to begin each day with drills and parade formations. These began at 7:00 A.M. and lasted for about an hour. "Initially," one woman marine recalled, "the male drill instructors were indignant to have been selected to teach drill to women. They showed us no mercy and taught us the same way as they did male recruits." At the end of the war the women were transferred to the inactive Marine Corps Reserve and were eventually discharged.

Women would not be enrolled in the corps again until World War II. As before, they were only allowed to join the Marine Corps Reserve. Ruth Cheney Streeter was one of the first women to enlist in the corps in World War II. She headed the Marine Corps Women's Reserve until the end of the war, ultimately attaining the rank of colonel. Nearly 19,000 women served in the reserves during the war—enough to free a division of men to fight overseas. They not only held jobs as clerks and nurses but also worked as parachute riggers, air control tower operators, and truck drivers. By the end of the war women were filling positions in 16 fields and more than 200 specialties.

After World War II, women were retained in the reserves, and in 1948 they were allowed to join the regular Marine Corps. Today, they can be found in every branch and occupation of the corps except one—the combat units of the infantry, artillery, armor, and aviation wings. The leadership of the Marine Corps does not yet feel that women marines should fight as combat soldiers.

By late 1988 there were 9,639 women in the Marine Corps, includ-

Brigadier General Gail Reals.

ing the corps's first woman general promoted to the rank by a marine promotion board. She is Brigadier General Gail Reals, who in 1985 beat out her male competitors for the coveted grade. As the commander of the 96-square-mile Marine Corps Base at Quantico, Virginia, she oversees 9,000 officers, enlisted marines, and civilians. Reals, who began her career as a private in the secretarial pool, is a dedicated marine officer for whom the corps seems like home. She says that career opportunities for women have gotten much better since she enlisted in 1955. "It's an uphill battle," she says of being a woman marine. "But the example I set can make marines aware of all the talent they have in the ranks."

and the army. The battle of Belleau Wood had received much favorable press in the United States, and army generals were unhappy about marine glory in a theater of war that normally belonged to the army. Many army generals argued that if the corps wanted to fight like the army it should be absorbed into the army and not be left as a separate branch of the armed forces. The officers of the Marine Corps argued strongly against having the corps taken over by the army, and under Lejeune they began to think about new roles for the marines.

In 1922, Lejeune stated that the Marine Corps should more fully develop its role as "a mobile . . . force adequate to conduct offensive land operations against hostile Naval bases." Even though it had assumed this role earlier in its history, this concept was new for the Marine Corps in the early 20th century. Since the end of the Civil War the corps had been called upon to defend American naval bases located outside the United States. It did not engage in prolonged and sustained offensive operations against strong enemy targets. Rather, it was used for short military campaigns and for longer occupations of militarily weak countries such as Haiti and Nicaragua. The expanded role that Lejeune envisioned called for a dramatically beefed-up corps—one that could fight a long military campaign against the best-trained forces of the most advanced nations of the world.

The one country that Lejuene and his lieutenants foresaw as a potential adversary was Japan. In 1905 the Japanese won a startling victory against Russia in a war fought for possession of Korea and Manchuria, which marked the beginning of Japan's imperial expansion throughout Asia. By the 1920s Japan not only had gained outright control of Korea and economic domination of Manchuria, it had also gained footholds on a number of strategic Pacific islands from which it could launch military operations in the event of war. In 1922 Lejeune sent one of his most trusted aides, Major Earl Ellis, on a secret spying mission to the Japanese-held Marshall Islands. Ellis never returned from this mission. He died under mysterious circumstances sometime in late 1922 or early 1923. But before his death Ellis dispatched reports back to Lejeune warning against Japanese intentions to fortify the Pacific islands. Throughout his career Ellis had stressed the need to train marines in the techniques of mass naval landings, which came to be called amphibious landings because the marines would be launched from navy ships at sea to fight on land.

During the 1920s the marines stepped up their efforts at perfecting new landing techniques. This was a difficult task, as the proper equipment to ferry troops from naval boats to the shore did not exist at the time. The corps developed several models of boats, but none worked as well as the senior officers had hoped. Also, tactical concepts had to be worked out from scratch

Major General John A. Lejeune, commandant of the Marine Corps from 1920 to 1929, was one of the corps's most forward-looking leaders. Under his command the marines assumed a larger role as a mobile assault force that could be launched from naval ships at sea to attack enemy bases on land.

In 1931 marines practice an amphibious landing along the shores of the Potomac River in Quantico, Virginia. The Marine Corps's efforts at perfecting amphibious landings would pay off several years later, when it repeatedly employed this tactic to begin its campaigns in the Pacific theater of World War II.

because amphibious landings of the magnitude and striking power proposed had never been attempted by the marines. The first large practice exercises in 1922 and 1925 were far from perfect: Forces landed on the wrong beaches; artillery support from ships offshore was sloppy and misdirected; and the landing craft used were not large or versatile enough to transport men, material, and equipment such as tanks and heavy artillery.

By 1933 many of the problems had been ironed out. That year the Marine Corps announced a new organizational unit that would continue to be a mainstay of the marines to the present day: the Fleet Marine Force. This force would consist of marine units of varying size carried aboard all ships of the U.S. Navy. The units would be on constant alert and ready to strike from the sea on short notice. By July 1935 the corps had produced a publication to instruct officers in the new techniques of amphibious warfare with which the marines had been experimenting during the previous decade. Entitled *Tentative*

Landing Operations Manual, it touched on all aspects of landing large numbers of marines from ships to shore: the need for air support; the coordination from shore of naval artillery gunfire; the importance of a clear, simple system of command; and the proper use of landing craft. By 1940 the corps had even perfected their landing craft. Called the LCVP (which stood for Landing Craft, Vehicle, Personnel), this vessel was a 36-foot boat with a retractable ramp on the bow. The ramp was raised when moving from ship to shore but could be lowered when the boat hit the beach. Once on the beach, as many as 50 marines could storm off each LCVP. A larger craft, called the LCM (which stood for Landing Craft Mechanized), was built to carry tanks. The corps was fortunate that it had this system in place by 1940, for on December 7, 1941, the Japanese attacked the U.S. naval base at Pearl Harbor, Hawaii, and the United States—and the Marine Corps—entered its second great worldwide conflict of the 20th century.

World War II

The strike on Pearl Harbor took the American military command by surprise. The Japanese knew that the U.S. fleet usually spent the weekends in port, and their Sunday morning attack caught many ships of America's Pacific Fleet in a vulnerable position. The Japanese sank five battleships and severely damaged three others. Fortunately, the aircraft carriers *Enterprise* and *Lexington* were at sea that Sunday, as were a number of other cruisers. Furthermore, the battleship *Colorado* was berthed in Bremerton, Washington, and the aircraft carrier *Saratoga* was in San Diego. These surviving ships were quickly assembled as the nucleus of the wartime American Pacific Fleet and plans were developed to counter the threat of further Japanese attacks.

Viewed dispassionately, the Japanese attack on Pearl Harbor was perplexing. The United States and Japan had been at odds over Japanese military aggression in China and threats to French and British colonial possessions in Southeast Asia, but the Japanese were far from sure that American citizens wanted to enter a war against Japan. The attack on Pearl Harbor ended any reluctance Americans had about war. From the moment the first bomb struck the first American ship, the American people were irrevocably committed to the defeat of Japan. On their part, the Japanese seemed to benefit only slightly from the attack, buying themselves time to complete their aggression in Asia. In short order they conquered French Indochina, Netherlands East Indies, and British Malaya, as well as the American colony of the Philippines. Yet, the time they had bought by the attack on Pearl Harbor was short. Within six months the U.S. Navy was back at sea. The navy turned back the Japanese at the Battle of the Coral Sea, off northern Australia, from May 4 to 8, 1942. One month later it defeated the Japanese naval forces at the Battle of Midway Island in the central Pacific. Both of these naval engagements were important because they established American control over the seas skirting the Japanese Pacific empire. Also, both were the first big sea battles in which aircraft mattered more than battleships. The days of artillery slugging matches between battleships were over; from 1942 on, whichever navy controlled the air from its aircraft carriers would also dominate the sea.

American military planners quickly decided that the Marine Corps was the ideal fighting force to carry the war to the Japanese in the Pacific. By midsummer the first marine division ever to be assembled had begun training

The USS Arizona *burns in its berth at the naval base in Pearl Harbor, Hawaii, after being hit by Japanese bombs on December 7, 1941. After the surprise attack, the more than 400 marines stationed at the base prepared for the return of the Japanese bombers. The next day the United States declared war on Japan.*

in New Zealand. (A division is made up of about 20,000 men.) The military had determined that it was going to work its way toward the Japanese islands via two routes. One would begin in the South Pacific and attack and destroy Japanese bases north of Australia. Once this was accomplished this force would push on to New Guinea and eventually would retake the Philippines. Vice Admiral Chester Ghormley was overall commander of this group, and the command of the amphibious forces was given to Rear Admiral Richmond Turner, a choice that dismayed the marines. Turner was a naval aviator who had no experience with amphibious operations. To help Turner with day-to-day decisions the Marine Corps appointed Major General Alexander Vandegrift, a veteran marine who had served in Nicaragua, Vera Cruz, Haiti, and China.

The other main American military force was assembled to strike in the central Pacific. The plans for this group called for it to island-hop across the Gilbert, Marshall, and Mariana island chains. From the Marianas the Army Air Forces could establish bases to bomb the cities of the main islands of Japan, and U.S. forces would mass in preparation for an invasion of Japan. The Second, Third, and Fourth marine divisions under the command of marine lieutenant general Holland "Howlin' Mad" Smith were mobilized for this second campaign. Vice Admiral Marc Mitscher had overall command of this group.

The first target of this two-pronged attack was an island in the South Pacific called Guadalcanal. Major General Vandegrift was ordered to begin assembling his men for training exercises in New Zealand in late June 1942. This gave the First Division only five weeks to prepare for the invasion—far too little time for the large, complex campaign that was to come, but American leaders insisted that the marines had to hit Guadalcanal before the Japanese had time to reinforce their own troops there. The invasion was code-named Operation Watchtower. Supported by 3 aircraft carriers, the 11,000 men of the First Division hit the beach at Guadalcanal in their new LCVPs on August 7, 1942. (The other 8,000 men were landed on a smaller island opposite Guadalcanal.) The first landing groups went ashore unopposed and quickly took the objectives assigned to them. However, the following waves, loaded with the provisions, equipment, and ammunition that would sustain the First Division during the next several months, became ensnarled in a gigantic mess on the beach. Fortunately, the Japanese forces on Guadalcanal were few and were not able to attack the marines at the beachhead immediately. Marine forces quickly took the airfield, their main objective. From there the Americans planned to base marine and navy pilots who would carry out bombing raids on the large Japanese base at Rabaul, located on the island of New Britain only 210 miles away.

The Pacific Theater, 1941–45

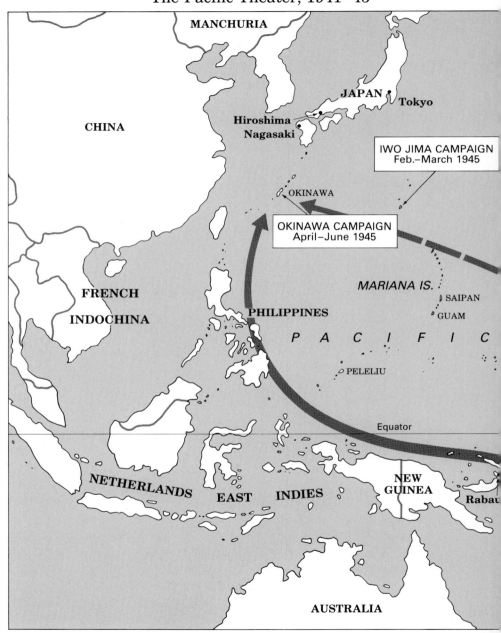

MANCHURIA

CHINA

JAPAN

Tokyo

Hiroshima
Nagasaki

IWO JIMA CAMPAIGN
Feb.–March 1945

OKINAWA

OKINAWA CAMPAIGN
April–June 1945

MARIANA IS.

SAIPAN

FRENCH

INDOCHINA

PHILIPPINES

GUAM

P A C I F I C

PELELIU

Equator

NETHERLANDS

EAST   INDIES

NEW
GUINEA

Rabau

AUSTRALIA

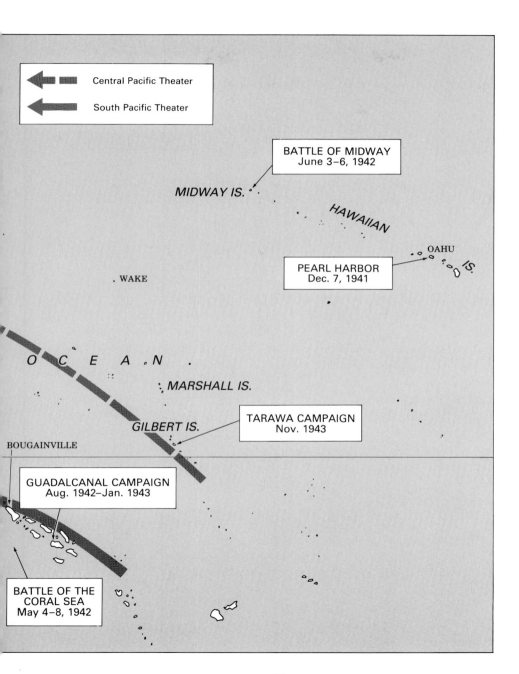

Central Pacific Theater

South Pacific Theater

BATTLE OF MIDWAY
June 3–6, 1942

MIDWAY IS.

HAWAIIAN

OAHU

PEARL HARBOR
Dec. 7, 1941

IS.

. WAKE

O C E A N

MARSHALL IS.

GILBERT IS.

TARAWA CAMPAIGN
Nov. 1943

BOUGAINVILLE

GUADALCANAL CAMPAIGN
Aug. 1942–Jan. 1943

BATTLE OF THE
CORAL SEA
May 4–8, 1942

Two days after the invasion, Vice Admiral Fletcher, commander of the naval support group, ordered the three aircraft carriers supporting the invasion to move away from Guadalcanal. These carriers were among the few the American forces possessed, and Fletcher was fearful of losing them to Japanese air attacks coming from Rabaul. Fletcher's move left the marines on Guadalcanal without adequate air support to prevent the Japanese from landing their own invasion force, which is precisely what the Japanese did. On August 18, 1,500 Japanese soldiers landed on both sides of the airfield, which had been renamed Henderson Field after a marine pilot killed at the Battle of Midway Island 2 months earlier. On the night of August 21 the Japanese tried to storm the airfield but were stopped by a marine unit at the stagnant, slime-covered Ilu River. The marines mowed down the Japanese as they tried to cross the river. The next day the rest of the Japanese force was trapped on the beach near the airfield, where it was decimated by a coordinated land and air attack. Eight hundred of the 1,500-man force were killed. The rest were either taken prisoner or escaped into the inhospitable jungle.

This setback did not stop the Japanese, who continued to send soldiers in piecemeal fashion to Guadalcanal. By October 1942 the Japanese had 20,000 men on the island. The marines had about the same number of men. Since the first attacks in August the two sides had been engaged in almost constant combat, but there had not yet been any knockout wins by either side. The marines still controlled Henderson Field, and the Japanese were kept at bay in the malaria-ridden lowlands. Both sides were exhausted, and the Japanese were increasingly desperate to finish the fight. Such stress might have caused an inexperienced group of soldiers to crumple. Even though the First Division had many new recruits, they were backed up by a cadre of lifetime marines, whom Colonel Samuel B. Griffith, Jr., called the "first sergeants yanked off 'planks' in Navy yards . . . gunnery sergeants who had fought in France, perennial privates with disciplinary records a yard long . . . the 'Old Breed' of the United States Marines." Griffith continued:

> They were inveterate gamblers and accomplished scroungers, who drank hair tonic in preference to post exchange beer, cursed with wonderful fluency, and never went to chapel unless forced to. . . . They knew their weapons and they knew their tactics. They were tough and they knew they were good. There were enough of them to leaven the Division and to impart to the thousands of younger men a share both in the unique spirit which they animated and the skills they possessed.

Troops disembark from their landing craft and storm the beach at Guadalcanal in August 1942. The marines' six-month battle for this island in the South Pacific was their first, as well as their longest, of World War II.

The First Division would need every drop of this spirit. On the night of October 27 the Japanese again tried to take Henderson Field, but they were repulsed in the single most bloody battle of the campaign. Two thousand Japanese were killed that day and the next, on a ridge that ran along one side of the field. This was to be the final major engagement of the Battle of Guadalcanal. Cutting their losses, the Japanese ordered a slow retreat from the island, and by late January 1943 the battle was over. The cost to the Japanese was staggering: 23,000 of their soldiers had been killed. The marines lost 1,200 men and 2,800 were wounded.

The Battle of Guadalcanal was the longest battle of the war for the Marine Corps, and it served notice to the Japanese that the marines were a force to be

A marine sharpshooter seeks cover behind a tree stump during the battle of Tarawa in November 1943. Although from the start things went wrong for the marines at Tarawa—their landing craft got caught on the coral reefs surrounding the atoll—the Americans ultimately routed the Japanese in a fierce 3-day battle that left nearly 1,000 marines dead.

reckoned with. Furthermore, it established the effectiveness of the marine air arm. The new F4U Corsairs that marine aviators had begun to fly proved a match for the Japanese Zeros. By February 1943 the marines had taken control of the sky and had begun to counterattack the Japanese base at Rabaul. The American advance in the South Pacific gathered momentum.

The next important battles for the marines occurred in the central Pacific. Relentlessly, the Second, Third, and Fourth marine divisions began their island-hopping campaign in late 1943. The idea of this operation was to skip areas of concentrated Japanese troop strength and hit points of weakness so that the strong areas would be cut off by the American advance and gradually wither as a result of a blockade imposed by American naval and air power. This idea had not yet been perfected by the time the first battle of this campaign was fought. This engagement, at the tiny atoll of Tarawa, was one of the most ferocious and, some critics say, the most unnecessary battle of the war. But the Japanese had constructed an airfield there that some American military leaders believed had to be captured if the marines were to continue their advance to Japan.

The marines came ashore at Tarawa on November 20, 1943. Through a combination of mishaps, 1,113 marines were killed and 2,290 were wounded in a fierce three and a half days of fighting. The Japanese had a small force on the island—only 5,000 troops—but they were well fortified and heavily armed with artillery. The American assault ran squarely into the heavily fortified Japanese positions. To further complicate matters, many of the American landing craft got stuck on coral reefs hundreds of yards from the beach. The first waves of marines never had a chance of success; they were slaughtered in their stalled landing craft or shot up on the beach. The American attack did not let up in spite of the losses suffered. Eventually, by sheer force of numbers and determination, the marines overwhelmed parts of the island and proceeded to the areas where their fellow marines were still pinned down. The Japanese soldiers fought them from bunker to bunker to the very end. Only 17 of the 5,000 Japanese soldiers had been taken prisoner by the end of the battle; all the others died fighting.

This action set the standard for the remaining battles in the Pacific. The Japanese were courageous and determined soldiers, but the marines were equally relentless. Robert Sherrod, a reporter for *Time* magazine, described them as fighting "almost solely on esprit de corps. . . . It was inconceivable to most Marines that they should let another Marine down. . . . The Marines simply assumed that they were the world's best fighting men."

By February 1944 the marines had island-hopped to the Marshall Islands in the central Pacific, and in July they took control of Saipan, in the Mariana Islands. From Saipan, American B-29 Superfortress bombers began day-and-night bombardment of Japanese cities. By early March 1945 the Army Air Forces were conducting regular bombing raids on Japanese cities. On one day alone, March 9, 1945, the air force dropped 1,665 tons of incendiary bombs on

Tokyo from their B-29s. (Incendiary bombs are designed to cause fire rather than to destroy targets by explosion.) This raid destroyed 16 square miles of Tokyo and killed more than 80,000 residents in a fire storm created by the bombardment.

In the meantime, the American ground forces were moving one step closer to Japan, waging a brutal battle for a tiny island named Iwo Jima. Iwo Jima was considered strategically important because it was only 670 miles from Tokyo— half the distance the B-29 bombers were flying from Saipan. Also, it could be used as a base for fighter planes escorting the B-29s as well as a place where crippled bombers could make emergency landings after bombing missions on Japan.

The invasion of Iwo Jima had begun on February 19, 1945, but the actual weakening of the Japanese hold on the island had started long before then. Prior to the invasion, marine and naval aircraft had bombed the island for 74 consecutive days. As in Tarawa, the enemy was well dug in. An elaborate system of interconnecting tunnels had been constructed, and the 23,000 Japanese defenders were heavily armed with 380 pieces of artillery and 22 tanks. Sixty thousand marines of the Third Division, Fourth Division, and the newly formed Fifth Division came ashore at Iwo Jima. The fighting was similar to what the marines had encountered on Tarawa: slow hand-to-hand combat to disengage the enemy from the caves and bunkers they had built; lots of artillery and mortar fire directed against the marines to make the going even more costly; and few prisoners taken by either side. But the marines were not to be stopped. The battle, for the most part, was over by April 1945. The marines were to lose more than 5,900 men, and 17,372 were wounded. Fewer than 1,100 Japanese soldiers were captured. The Battle of Iwo Jima was, in General Holland Smith's words, "the most savage and costly battle in the history of the Marine Corps. . . . [I]t has few parallels in military annals."

U.S. military leaders felt they had to take one last island before launching an invasion of Japan itself. This island was Okinawa, situated only 350 miles off the southern tip of Japan.

The battle for Okinawa was the last of the conflicts in the Pacific theater. It was also the largest, involving 548,000 troops from all of the American armed forces. A few days before the April 1 invasion, Japanese *kamikaze* (suicide) pilots began an assault on the invasion fleet stationed off the island, attempting to crash their planes into the American ships. (By the end of the battle kamikazes would succeed in sinking 34 U.S. ships and damaging 288 others.) On April 1, Easter Sunday, a combined landing force of army troops and marines from the First Division and the new Sixth Division stormed the west

Marines carefully inch their way up the beach of Iwo Jima as smoke from fighting around Mount Suribachi drifts skyward in the background. About 60,000 marines came ashore at Iwo Jima, which was, in the words of one former marine general, "the most savage and costly battle in the history of the Marine Corps."

coast of Okinawa. At the same time marines from the Second Division landed on the southeastern coast to divert attention away from the main invasion force. The Japanese had chosen to hold their fire until the Americans were no longer protected by their naval and air support, and the main landing force met little resistance. The marines took their objective, the mountainous northern part of the island, and were soon called on to help the army forces, which were meeting stiff opposition in the south. The Japanese commander, Lieutenant General Mitsuru Ushijima, had set up his troops in three defensive lines, taking advantage of the ridges that ran across the island to provide a natural barrier against the invading Americans. His forces were well dug into the numerous caves that punctuated the ridges. The marines faced one of their toughest struggles in taking a rectangular-shaped mound dubbed Sugar Loaf Hill. For nine days in early May control of the hill seesawed between the Japanese forces and the men of the Sixth Division. The marines were finally victorious, but the contest cost them 2,662 men. By the end of May, Lieutenant General Ushijima was forced to pull his troops back to the third ridge. This final stronghold, Kunishi Ridge, promised to be another bloody confrontation. From June 11 to June 16 the two sides battled furiously for the ridge, and by June 21 the last of the Japanese forces on Okinawa had been defeated.

Mamoru Shigemitsu (seated), the Japanese foreign minister, signs the formal surrender aboard the USS Missouri *on September 2, 1945, ending the war with Japan. American general Douglas MacArthur, the supreme commander of the Allied forces, broadcasts the ceremonies over a microphone.*

After Okinawa was taken, the American troops in the Pacific prepared to invade Japan. Military strategists projected that this campaign would involve approximately 1 million servicemen and cost an estimated 100,000 American lives. But the invasion was never carried out. On August 6, 1945, the Army Air Forces dropped an atomic bomb on Hiroshima. Three days later a second A-bomb was dropped on Nagasaki. On August 10 the Japanese asked for peace, and the bloodiest war in marine history was over. Nearly 20,000 marines had been killed and 67,207 had been wounded.

In a span of 25 years the United States had fought and won 2 world wars. The dedication and spirit of the United States Marines had contributed immeasurably to the outcome of these wars. The United States came out of World War II as the premier economic and military power in the world. It seemed certain that the 20th century was destined to be, in the words of publisher Henry Luce, the "American Century."

Marines in Vietnam move a 105-millimeter howitzer—a type of cannon—into position in September 1968. By November 1968 marine strength in Vietnam had peaked at 85,000 men and women.

FIVE

Worldwide Commitments

During World War II the strength of the Marine Corps grew to an all-time high of 485,000 men and women. In the late 1940s elements of the corps could now be found scattered around the world and were especially prominent in the Pacific basin as a result of America's victory. The United States was now the leading world military power, and American political leaders decided to build a network of military bases around the globe so that a permanent structure would be in place to enforce peace and preserve American gains bought at so high a price during the war. Marines were to be stationed at many of these bases. In Asia the United States would maintain permanent marine bases in Japan and Okinawa, and, along with other U.S. forces, marines would maintain a presence in the Philippines and Korea. These permanent American outposts in the Pacific would guarantee that the United States would not be caught unprepared by an aggressor nation as it had been at the start of World War II.

The Marine Corps had undergone significant changes as a result of the war. Black Americans were admitted into the corps for the first time during World War II. This new policy was the result of President Franklin D. Roosevelt's Executive Order 8802 of 1941, which decreed that special units should be established for black marines. This order did not completely integrate the corps—that would come in 1948 through an executive order by President

Harry S. Truman—but it made the important statement that no institution of American public life should discriminate against any American citizen because of race.

The Marine Corps was also affected by the National Security Act of 1947, which reorganized the entire American military structure. The act brought all of the armed forces together under one cabinet-level department called the National Military Establishment (renamed the Department of Defense in 1949). The existing War Department and Navy Department were retained as separate branches within the National Military Establishment, with the War Department assuming the new name of the Department of the Army. A third branch, the Department of the Air Force, was created out of what had been the Army Air Forces. The act reaffirmed the Marine Corps's relationship with the U.S. Navy and formally recognized the corps's role as an elite amphibious force attached to the navy. According to the law the commandant of the Marine Corps would report to the chief of naval operations, who in turn would report to the secretary of the navy, a civilian appointed by the president. This meant that the commandant was, in effect, subordinate to the navy's highest-ranking officer, a point that rankled many marines.

It was impossible to maintain the high level of troop strength the Marine Corps had reached during World War II. Most of the volunteers who had entered the corps during the war were now desperately eager to return to civilian life. By July 1947 demobilization had reduced the corps to 92,000 men and women. In spite of this rapid reduction of troops, the corps was not neglected after World War II as it had been after almost every other war in U.S. history. As a result of the United States's new position as the preeminent world power, Americans possessed a new awareness about their place in the world and the need for military readiness. Also, Americans perceived a threat to their security coming from the only other military superpower to have emerged from the war: the Soviet Union.

Postwar, peacetime Marine Corps troop strength was authorized by Congress at approximately 100,000 men and women—about four times the strength of the corps before the war. Even at full strength the corps could not ignore the existence of what was perhaps the most radical innovation ever introduced into warfare: the atomic bomb. The dilemma for the corps and the other military services was to figure out how they could remain effective fighting forces if potential enemies possessed atomic weapons. Clearly, large masses of troops were vulnerable to atomic attack, and in World War II the corps had relied on large mass invasions to achieve its objectives. The leadership of the corps had to rethink the strategies and tactics that had enabled the marines to be successful in the last war.

The answer to this problem seemed to come in another new invention: the helicopter. The helicopter was perfected just before World War II by a Russian-born American engineer named Igor Sikorsky, but the flaws in its design were not remedied before the end of the war. Even though the first helicopters were flown by the army on experimental rescue and observation missions in 1944 and 1945, the helicopter was widely available to the military only after the war. The Marine Corps quickly embraced the helicopter. Here was an aircraft that was able to take off vertically from the deck of an aircraft carrier—or even a smaller ship—and transport troops as far as 100 miles away.

In 1951 a huge Sikorsky helicopter drops supplies for marines fighting on the Korean front. The helicopter revolutionized the way the marines fought their battles: Not only could it ferry supplies and ammunition to marines in remote places, but it could also transport troops in and out of war zones in an extremely short period of time.

A helicopter not only could land on a beach but could also touch down in a small area where a conventional plane was unable to land. It could ferry supplies, artillery, ammunition, and equipment, as well as evacuate the wounded and quickly supply reinforcements. And above all, it could do all this from a distance and in such a way that troop concentrations could be dispersed and assembled rapidly. Because of this mobility, troops would be more difficult targets for an atomic attack. The marines worked out a new concept for hitting their enemies with a helicopter assault; they called it vertical envelopment. This strategy would play an increasingly important role in the 25 years after World War II.

Cold War and Stalemate

American optimism following World War II soon faded. On June 25, 1950, the army of Communist North Korea launched a surprise attack on the Republic of South Korea. This attack was partly the result of the confused signals American leaders were giving about South Korea's place in the U.S. defense scheme in the Pacific. In June 1949 the U.S. military had withdrawn the last of its forces from South Korea, leaving only 500 military advisers to train the South Korean army. In January 1950 American secretary of state Dean Acheson defined the areas that the U.S. government considered worthy of defending. This zone, the outer edge of America's long-range defense perimeter, did not include South Korea. Because of these statements and actions on the part of the U.S. government, the North Koreans must have assumed that the United States would not act to defend South Korea from a North Korean attack. They were wrong in this assumption.

Within a month the North Koreans had succeeded in completely overrunning the army of South Korea. They bottled up the South Koreans and their American army and marine reinforcements—which had been sent in shortly after the invasion—in the southeast corner of the country. The Americans and South Koreans desperately began to form a defensive perimeter that would protect them from the North Korean soldiers while they waited for further troop reinforcements from a combined United Nations force. By August 1950 enough troops had been sent to stop the North Korean advance, although the South Koreans, the Americans, and their UN allies were still squeezed into a small area of southeastern Korea.

The overall commander of the UN forces in Korea was General Douglas MacArthur, the army general who had been put in charge of the American

Korea, 1950–53

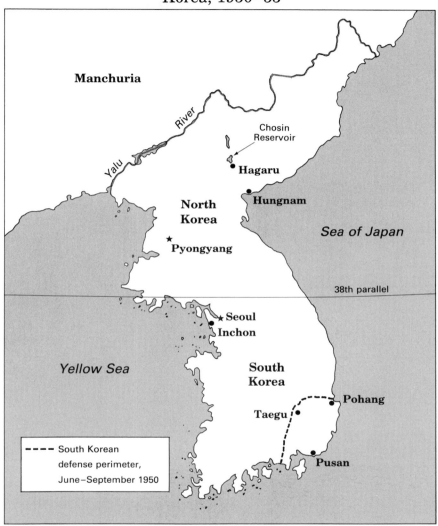

occupation of Japan after World War II. By August MacArthur had devised a daring scheme to counterattack the North Koreans. The First Marine Division, the unit that had served so resolutely in Guadalcanal and elsewhere during World War II, was to lead an amphibious assault deep behind enemy lines. This invasion, which was targeted to come ashore at Inchon, near the South Korean capital of Seoul, would cut off the majority of the North Korean troops, who were concentrated around the pocket of American and South Korean troops far to the south. After isolating and destroying the North Korean forces, MacArthur envisioned an easy campaign to take North Korea, thus uniting the entire Korean Peninsula under the pro-American South Korean government.

The invasion itself was tricky, owing to the extreme tidal changes at Inchon. The tides there were high enough to allow invasion craft to land on only three days of the month. Furthermore, the tides during these three days reached the depth to allow craft to land only for three hours in the morning and three hours in the afternoon. This left little room for error on the part of the First Marine Division; the invasion had to be impeccably planned and executed. Troops of the first few waves had to hit the beach exactly at the right time and were

Marines patrol a devastated area near Inchon, Korea, soon after executing a daring amphibious assault there on September 15, 1950. The operation, which took place deep within enemy territory, effectively cut off the North Korean forces concentrated in the southeast corner of the country and opened the way for a South Korean offensive in North Korea.

under great pressure to seize their initial targets quickly. The next waves, coming in the afternoon, were to bring vital reinforcements, munitions, and supplies to propel the invasion inland. If anything went wrong in any phase of the invasion the whole plan could come apart.

The First Division hit the beach during the early morning of September 15, 1950, and quickly took the weakly defended enemy positions that overlooked the invasion site. After dozens of invasions during World War II, the First Division was one of the most experienced amphibious units in the world; their training and the confidence that came with it stood them well at Inchon. The succeeding waves came ashore with no hitch, and the town of Inchon was captured within a day and a half. The North Koreans had been taken completely by surprise. By September 29 the marines had not only established a beachhead at Inchon, but they had pushed inland and taken the South Korean capital of Seoul as well. By mid-October—only two and a half weeks after Seoul fell—the North Korean forces in South Korea had been routed, and MacArthur began his advance into North Korea.

President Truman's advisers were divided about whether U.S. forces should advance into North Korea, but finally Truman made the decision to proceed northward. As MacArthur had anticipated, the marines—now with army reinforcements—met little resistance in the north. A large part of the North Korean army had been destroyed, and the Koreans had no air force, so American control of the skies was complete. By Thanksgiving Day 1950 the Americans and their allies were nearing the Yalu River, the dividing line between Korea and Communist China. The Chinese had warned the Americans that they would not tolerate the conquest of North Korea. They viewed Communist North Korea as a buffer between themselves and American forces in South Korea, and they did not want to lose this zone because it would expose them directly to an American military invasion. The Chinese, realizing that their hold over North Korea was collapsing, struck against the Americans on November 27, four days after Thanksgiving.

The Chinese attack surprised the Americans as much as the American attack at Inchon had surprised the North Koreans. A large part of the First Marine Division was trapped deep inside North Korea, at a place called the Chosin Reservoir. Cold and hungry, running out of ammunition, and freezing in the first blast of the bitter Korean winter, these marines were squeezed into a small perimeter around the town of Hagaru and were pinned down there for more than a week. On December 4, 1950, they launched a daring breakout and fought their way down the highway from the mountains to the coastal town of Hungnam, where they were evacuated by American ships to safer positions in

South Korea. From 1951 until 1953 the war in Korea raged inconclusively along the 38th parallel. General MacArthur wanted to use American atomic weapons for another assault on North Korea, but President Truman vetoed this idea and removed MacArthur from his command. Both sides finally realized that they could gain nothing further from the war. On July 17, 1953, representatives of the UN and Communist forces signed a truce that ended the fighting and recognized a boundary between North and South Korea that ran roughly along the 38th parallel. The Korean War was over.

The Korean War was unique in that it was the first time jet combat airplanes and helicopters had been used on a large scale. Helicopters were especially important in evacuating wounded marines and stringing communications lines over rugged mountainous terrain. These aircraft were not quite so important yet in moving large numbers of combat troops from one spot to another because they were not big enough or powerful enough to carry more than a few soldiers at a time.

Perhaps the most important lesson the United States learned in Korea was that, although it was willing and able to defend its Asian allies, even with its tremendous power complete victory could not be assured where political objectives were set at something less than total victory.

The rest of the 1950s was a time of relative calm for the Marine Corps. The United States had entered a period of tense standoff with the Soviet Union and its Communist allies in China and Eastern Europe. This era, which was characterized by deep mistrust between the Soviet Union and the United States, was known as the cold war. It was thus termed because, even though no military campaigns were waged between the two nations, the tensions between them ran so high that active warfare almost broke out on several occasions. Rather than fighting each other directly, the United States and the Soviet Union engaged in unceasing propaganda attacks on each other. The Soviets promised to "bury" the United States, and America directed frequent, uncomplimentary radio broadcasts into Eastern Europe and the Soviet Union. The two sides also fought each other through proxies. In 1964, for example, a power struggle in the Congo (now Zaire) pitted the American-backed forces of Prime Minister Moise Tshombe against the Communist-supported rebel army led by Pierre Mulele and Christophe Gbenye. And in the 1950s, 1960s, and 1970s, the United States and the Soviet Union faced off from a distance in the struggle between Communist North Vietnam and American-backed South Vietnam.

Although the United States had been involved in events in Vietnam since 1950—providing arms and advice to French and South Vietnamese forces—the conflict escalated in the mid-1960s to include troops of the United States

U.S. marines brace against freezing temperatures and snow in the Chosin Reservoir region of North Korea. A surprise attack by the Chinese army on November 26, 1950, left marines of the First Division stranded in the mountainous area for more than a week. However, the marines valiantly fought their way down the mountain and were rescued by American ships along the coast.

Marines. (Several marine helicopter squadrons had been in Vietnam as early as 1962, lending operational support by ferrying supplies and troops, but they saw no combat action.) From 1960 to 1965 most of the fighting in South Vietnam was between the army of South Vietnam and a group of South Vietnamese Communist guerrillas known as the Vietcong. By 1965, however, large numbers of soldiers of the army of North Vietnam had entered into the conflict. The corrupt and unstable South Vietnamese government, which was having difficulty in winning battles against the Vietcong and the North Vietnamese, called on the United States to help by sending in U.S. combat soldiers. President Lyndon Johnson responded by dispatching both army and marine units: the marines being sent primarily to the northern part of Vietnam and the army to the southern part. The Ninth Marine Expeditionary Brigade was sent to Da Nang, and the Third Expeditionary Brigade was sent to Chu Lai. The marines were to guard airfields at both bases and to begin patrols to hunt down the North Vietnamese units in the provinces around these bases.

Marines of the Ninth Marine Expeditionary Brigade come ashore at Da Nang, Vietnam, on March 8, 1965. Some 5,000 marines landed that day—the first marine combat troops to be deployed in Vietnam. Less than four months later the number of marines in Vietnam had more than tripled.

The first marines, some 5,000 men of the Ninth Expeditionary Brigade, arrived in Vietnam on March 8, 1965. The marine ground forces were supported by marine air groups (using mostly A-4 Skyhawk jet fighter-bombers) and helicopter squadrons. The buildup of marine forces was rapid. By late June 1965, 16,000 marines were in Vietnam. One year later, in September 1966, 60,000 marines had landed, and by November 1968, marine strength there had peaked at 85,000.

The war in Vietnam was frustrating for the marines. Unlike their experience in the Pacific island-hopping campaigns during World War II—or even their combat against the North Koreans during the Korean War—the marines encountered no easily identifiable enemy in Vietnam. The Communist soldiers were difficult to pin down on the battlefield. This was a guerrilla war: The enemy, whether it was the Vietcong or the North Vietnamese army, used hit-and-run tactics and avoided large, fixed battles against the Americans. The Communists knew they would lose if they fought conventional land battles. The American forces possessed too much firepower, and the Communists had too little. Instead, the Communists concentrated their attacks against isolated targets all across Vietnam. Their tactics were to hit a unit, outpost, airbase, or artillery site hard for a few hours or days—perhaps even weeks—then to melt back into the countryside as soon as large numbers of reinforcements arrived. Thus, the Americans were continually bled of strength. They were never defeated outright in large engagements on the field, but they suffered small defeats on patrol. Gradually, as the North Vietnamese sent more troops to South Vietnam, the cost of maintaining an American presence in Vietnam grew. By September 1966, 1,700 marines had been killed in Vietnam; 9,000 had been wounded. During 1967, 3,452 more marines were killed and 35,994 were wounded. Because American forces could show no clear gains to compensate for these losses, public opinion in the United States began to shift against continuing the war.

The marines constructed a series of artillery bases in the northern part of South Vietnam. From these sites they received artillery support for their sweeps through the countryside. They called these sweeps their clear-and-hold strategy, whereby the marines attempted to clear an area of countryside of Communist guerrillas and then hold it for a while—a week, for instance, perhaps even a month. During this time the marine and civilian counterinsurgency experts could lecture the villagers through interpreters about the evils of communism and explain the details of nonexistent South Vietnamese land redistribution programs. In the meantime the other marines looked for Communist troops. But it was often impossible to tell Communists

A marine searches for Vietcong soldiers in the dense jungles of Vietnam. Unlike previous wars, where the U.S. forces faced their opponents in large land battles, the conflict in Vietnam was a guerrilla war in which the enemy carried out surprise attacks on isolated targets and then quickly melted back into the countryside.

from ordinary civilians—and often the ordinary civilians were Communists. Frequently the marines did not know whether they were dealing with friendly or unfriendly Vietnamese until it was too late. Sometimes they did not wait to find out.

The war in Vietnam climaxed in 1968, when U.S. forces faced their most severe test from the Vietcong and the North Vietnamese army. During late December 1967 and early January 1968 about six divisions of North Vietnamese troops had assembled in South Vietnam. On January 20 the North Vietnamese attacked Khe Sanh, a large marine base located on a strategic plateau in the northern part of South Vietnam. By the following day large units of North Vietnamese troops had managed to cut Khe Sanh off from all but air support. General William Westmoreland, the overall American commander in Vietnam, rushed in army and marine units in an effort to open up the roads to Khe Sanh. The deployment of troops may have been exactly what the North Vietnamese wanted, because it removed many soldiers from their regular positions. On January 30 the Vietcong and North Vietnamese forces launched a ferocious attack on almost every major city and base in South Vietnam. This attack, known as the Tet Offensive because it occurred during the Vietnamese New Year celebrations called Tet, stunned the American military establishment and shocked Americans in the United States. During the offensive the Vietcong penetrated the U.S. embassy compound in Saigon; they overran a number of provincial capitals and took the important city of Hue in the northern part of South Vietnam. For more than a month a fierce battle raged in Hue between the marines and the North Vietnamese, who had established a strong position in the ancient citadel at the center of the city.

While the marines and the North Vietnamese faced off in Hue, the battle for Khe Sanh continued. Repeated air strikes by American B-52 bombers and continual air reinforcements saved the base. The battle was declared officially over on April 14, 1968. Two hundred five Americans died at Khe Sanh and another 142 were killed at Hue. More than 2,000 were wounded in the 2 battles. The number of North Vietnamese casualties was impossible to determine, but U.S. estimates place the figure at about 20,000 at Khe Sanh alone.

As the casualties on both sides mounted, the American people began to withdraw their support for the conflict. Worried by the political consequences of this increasing opposition, U.S. government leaders revised their objectives. Victory was no longer the ultimate goal; obtaining a reasonable peace settlement was. The government's changing policies and the public's changing attitudes affected the marines in Vietnam. Unable to pursue a course of victory, their role in the conflict became more and more obscured. Negative public opinion further eroded the marines' sense of purpose about the war and contributed to a growing disillusionment among the troops.

The war in Vietnam began to wind down in 1969, when Richard M. Nixon was elected president. Nixon realized that the United States could not win the conflict under the political constraints that surrounded the war: That is, the United States could not win the war without invading North Vietnam. And even if the United States did launch an invasion it still could not win, because such a move would almost certainly mean a war with China and perhaps the Soviet Union. Not wanting to start a third world war and unable to decisively defeat the Communists in South Vietnam, Nixon slowly began withdrawing American forces. This process was called "Vietnamization," which meant that the United States turned the fighting of the war over to its South Vietnamese allies. The United States would still supply the weapons, but it would no longer send its own troops into what seemed to be a never-ending standoff. The last marine ground forces left Vietnam on June 25, 1971. After that only several thousand marine advisers remained to train South Vietnamese soldiers.

The South Vietnamese could not hold out very long against the Communists. Their troops were led for the most part by corrupt officers, and the government was not interested in creating democratic institutions. The people of South Vietnam lost faith in their rulers, and many of them apparently preferred the Communists to the government supported by the United States. The end finally came with a North Vietnamese offensive in the spring of 1975.

On April 29, with North Vietnamese armies surrounding Saigon, U.S. Marines guarding the American embassy carried out Operation Frequent Wind, evacuating the last Americans from South Vietnam.

For the marines the conflict in Vietnam was the first true helicopter war. Both marine and army units depended on helicopters to move them around the country, like pieces on a chessboard, in efforts to trap the slippery Communist units. Helicopters had become big enough now—and there were enough of them—to transport large numbers of men rapidly over impenetrable jungles and mountains. Vertical envelopment became a reality in Vietnam. Yet it did not work terribly well against a guerrilla army. Much more important than

U.S. civilians and pro-American South Vietnamese citizens hasten to board a Marine Corps helicopter during the fall of Saigon on April 29, 1975. More than 1,300 Americans and 1,500 Vietnamese were evacuated from Saigon on that day, in what was known as Operation Frequent Wind.

100

marine tactics were real political and social reforms on the part of the South Vietnamese government. But these reforms, when they came at all, were too little and too late to win the struggle.

Parade Rest: The Marines After Vietnam

The sour outcome of the war in Vietnam caused many Americans to reassess their convictions and those of the nation. More than 13,000 marines had been killed in the war, and 88,000 had been wounded. No longer were Americans eager to plunge into military adventures abroad. The conflict in Vietnam had clearly demonstrated that there were limits to American power. This reevaluation of America's role in the world had a corresponding effect on the Marine Corps.

In 1975, at the urging of the Senate Armed Services Committee, the new commandant of the Marine Corps, General Louis Wilson, ordered a thorough reexamination of the corps. Confidence in the Marine Corps had been shaken as a result of the Vietnam War. The marines had not made a major amphibious assault since the Inchon landing in 1950, and questions were raised about the corps's role as an elite amphibious assault organization. Furthermore, congressional leaders were disturbed by the apparent breakdown of discipline within the corps during the war and by the high incidence of desertion and drug addiction among corps members. This top-to-bottom review was to be conducted by a panel appointed by General Wilson. Named the Haynes Board after its chairman, Marine Corps major general Fred Haynes, the board was charged with assessing the relevance of the marines and proposing ways to strengthen the corps as it began its third century of service to the country.

Some critics suggested that the Marine Corps should become a Pacific theater force exclusively, that it should leave all European and Middle East combat roles to the army. Others wondered whether the corps had enough firepower to meet an enemy on the modern battlefield. And inevitably, questions were raised about marine morale. In 1976 the Haynes Board recommended that the marines not be restricted to any one theater of action. The corps was seen basically as the rapid-response force of the U.S. military and it should be ready to respond quickly to trouble anywhere in the world. The board also recommended strengthening the marine recruiting program. As a result of these recommendations and the corps's own reassessment of its mission and practices, several thousand "problem marines" were dismissed from service, and the corps issued new guidelines stipulating that 75 percent

Marines patrol the streets of Grenville, Grenada, in October 1983. The marines were dispatched to Grenada when leaders of several neighboring Caribbean nations asked for American assistance to quell a Communist rebellion on the tiny island.

of its enlisted personnel be high school graduates. It also took steps to clean up the mistreatment of recruits at the training camps at Parris Island, South Carolina, and in San Diego, California. Over a period of several years several hundred drill instructors at both locations were punished for their brutal treatment of recruits. Even though marine training is still rough, these actions went a long way toward restoring the public's confidence in the corps and the corps's confidence in itself.

During the 1970s and 1980s the Marine Corps gradually rebuilt itself from the debacle of Vietnam. In 1983 the marines were again in the public eye as back-to-back events in faraway places shocked and saddened Americans. On October 23 the Marine Corps barracks in Beirut, Lebanon, was destroyed by a lone terrorist. Two days later a relief force of marines bound for Lebanon was called into action on the tiny Caribbean island of Grenada. Only days earlier Maurice Bishop, the prime minister of Grenada, had been murdered by the Grenadian military in a violent overthrow of the Socialist government. Leaders of neighboring Caribbean nations, fearful of a growing Communist presence in the region, asked the United States to assist a small force of troops from six Caribbean countries in restoring order to the island.

In the early hours of October 25, 400 U.S. Marines were helicoptered to Pearls Airport on the east coast of Grenada with orders to take the airstrip. Within two hours the lightly held airport was under marine control. That evening a second force of 250 marines stormed the beach at Grand Mal, on the west coast of Grenada, to rescue about 1,000 American citizens, most of whom were medical students at a local university. The marines encountered heavy fire from the Grenadian soldiers and their Cuban allies, whose forces were concentrated north of the capital of St. George's. The next day the marines secured the governor's residence, evacuating the governor general, while a combined army and marine force coming up from the south freed the besieged medical students. The marines continued to meet small pockets of resistance for several more days, but by October 31 the rebellion had been quelled and they were withdrawn from the island. Troops from the army's Eighty-second Airborne Division were brought in to maintain stability. By Christmas 1983 they, too, had been recalled, and only a skeleton group of military police and support troops remained to train Grenada's small security force.

Peacekeepers and Power: Beirut and the Persian Gulf

The Marine Corps was again called on to lend support during the Persian Gulf crises of 1987 and 1988. During these two years fighting between Iran and Iraq over control of the Shatt-al-Arab waterway, which divides the two countries, reached its greatest intensity. In many ways the war between Iran and Iraq was similar to World War I. Both sides charged each other against static

The USS Ford *(foreground), an American guided-missile frigate, escorts a Kuwaiti oil tanker through the Persian Gulf in October 1987. When Iran began attacking the ships of neutral Arab countries during the war between Iran and Iraq, the United States stepped in, providing a small naval fleet, which included marines, to protect tankers and ensure the free flow of oil out of the gulf.*

defenses backed up by tanks and heavy artillery, and both sides suffered huge casualties as a result of these outdated tactics. By 1987 the war had reached a stalemate, and in desperation Iraq began attacking the Iranian army with chemical weapons. This was the first time since World War I that any nation had used chemical weapons, and the Iraqi attacks shocked people all over the world.

To strike back against Iraq, Iran threatened to close the Persian Gulf to all ship traffic. It backed these threats by attacking oil tankers leaving the neutral ports of the Arab countries on the western side of the gulf. Iraqi air attacks on Iran were economically strangling Iranian oil shipping facilities, and Iran saw no other alternative but to try to choke off oil shipments from Kuwait, Saudi Arabia, and the United Arab Emirates. After all, much of the money from this oil was being used by the Arabs to fund Iraq's war with Iran.

When the Iranians began attacking the tankers of neutral Arabian countries, the United States stepped in to protect the shipment of oil out of the gulf. The Americans did this for two reasons: First, the free flow of oil out of the Persian Gulf was in the American national interest. Much of this oil was going to the United States, and most of the rest of it was destined for America's allies in Asia and Europe. Second, from the first days of the republic the United States has insisted on the right of all neutral nations to expect that their ships can sail freely and without fear of attack on the oceans of the world. The Iranians, by attacking ships in the Persian Gulf, violated this principle of the freedom of navigation, and the United States vigorously protested by taking direct action to ensure that shipping would not be stopped.

The United States sent a small fleet of destroyers and cruisers to the gulf to escort oil tankers into and out of the war zone. The Marine Corps played a small but significant role in this mission. Marines waited aboard an amphibious assault ship, the *Guadalcanal*, in the Persian Gulf and were ready at a moment's notice to attack Iranian missile sites there if the Iranians launched an all-out attack on American ships in the gulf war zone. Also, marine helicopter pilots based on U.S. warships in the gulf were involved in patrol duty and from time to time engaged Iranian patrol boats in exchanges of missile fire. During these actions several Iranian patrol boats were sunk by American helicopters.

In August 1988 the war in the gulf ended with a cease-fire between the Iranian and Iraqi forces. Thirty-nine Americans were killed in the conflict, 37 of whom died when Iraq inadvertently attacked an American frigate in May 1987. The frigate, the *Stark*, was seriously damaged when a missile from an Iraqi warplane struck the ship while it was on patrol duty in the Persian Gulf. And in April 1988 two marine pilots were killed when their helicopter was downed by the Iranians.

American forces had managed to walk a fine line during the Persian Gulf tanker war. They kept the sea lanes open without embroiling themselves in a larger war with Iran. This was achieved by applying the minimum amount of force necessary to daunt Iranian attacks. The Persian Gulf conflict can be viewed as a great success for the United States precisely because the American forces stationed in the Arabian Sea never had to be called into action.

In addition to developing fighting skills, such as marksmanship, marine recruits must pass rigorous physical tests to increase strength and build confidence as part of their basic training. Both men and women recruits must successfully complete 11 weeks of basic training at one of the Marine Corps's 2 recruit depots in the United States.

SIX

The Marine Corps and the Department of Defense

W hen President Harry S. Truman signed into law the National Security Act of 1947, which rearranged the military services into the organization that exists today, the command structure of the armed forces was integrated into a single unit under the Joint Chiefs of Staff. This group was initially composed of the chiefs of staff of the army and the air force and the chief of naval operations. Excluded from the group was the commandant of the Marine Corps. The corps lobbied hard for the inclusion of its leader on the Joint Chiefs, and in 1952 the commandant was allowed to participate in meetings in which the Marine Corps was concerned. But it would be another 26 years until the commandant was given full voting membership on the Joint Chiefs of Staff.

The command structure of the Department of Defense (DOD) is complex, but basically it works as follows. The head of the DOD, the secretary of defense, is a civilian cabinet-level officer appointed by the president and confirmed by the Senate. Under the secretary of defense are three major civilian aides: the secretary of the air force, the secretary of the army, and the secretary of the navy. The budgets, assignments and promotions of personnel, war planning, and requests for new military hardware for the marines and the navy are coordinated and directed by the secretary of the navy. The commanding officer in charge of the navy is the chief of naval operations; the commanding officer in charge of the marines is the commandant, who is on equal footing with the chief of naval operations.

The system of individual ranking in the marines is similar to that used in the army. Personnel are divided into two broad categories: enlisted personnel and officers. (In 1989 more than 197,000 men and women were enrolled in the corps: 20,000 officers and 177,271 enlisted personnel.) The ranking system is used to ensure an efficiently run military organization. Marines of lower rank are always under the command of and subject to the orders of those of higher ranks. The ranks for enlisted personnel run from private, the lowest-ranking marine, to corporal to sergeant. Sergeants in many ways are the marines who constitute the backbone of the corps. As the top-ranking enlisted personnel, they are in charge of supervising the actions of the men and women below them in rank, the corporals and privates who constitute the majority of the corps. Even though sergeants are outranked by even the lowest-ranking officer, they frequently have more experience and practical expertise than any other group in the marines.

The ranks of officers begin with lieutenants and move in ascending order to captain, major, lieutenant colonel, colonel, brigadier general, major general, lieutenant general, and general. All marine officers enter the officer rank at the lowest rung, as first lieutenant. Most officers enter the corps in one of three ways: by graduating from the U.S. Naval Academy at Annapolis, Maryland; by attending a Reserve Officers' Training Corps (ROTC) program at a college that offers the program; or by attending the Officer Training School in Quantico, Virginia, that is run by the Marine Corps.

The principle of civilian control of the military is built into the system of the National Security Act. What is extraordinary and important about this principle is the idea that the military must never be allowed to make decisions on its own that affect the fate of the American people. As the elected representatives of the people, the president, through the secretary of defense, and the Congress, through its committees, are the only people vested with the power to make decisions about American military policy. Civilian leaders decide what the military will do; once that decision has been made, the military leaders advise the civilian leaders on the best way to achieve their goals. This principle has been an important part of U.S. democracy since the writing of the Constitution. It is one of the crucial checks on the potential power of the military that

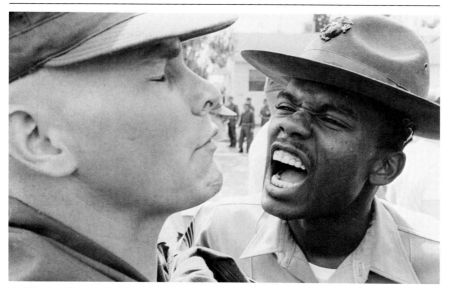

A Marine Corps drill instructor indoctrinates a recruit in the ways of the Marine Corps at the recruit depot in San Diego, California. After successfully completing basic training, a recruit undergoes several weeks of additional training for a Military Occupational Specialty (MOS), a specific job within the corps that will become the marine's specialty.

distinguishes American democracy from the systems of government of other nations. The most important result of this check is that, unlike the situation in other nations, the U.S. military has never tried to take over the government.

The Fleet Marine Force and the Marine Air-Ground Task Force

Today the basic unit of marine organization is still the Fleet Marine Force, the concept that was introduced during the 1930s. The Fleet Marine Force is the striking unit of the United States Marines, and elements of this force are carried aboard the U.S. naval fleet. Currently, the Fleet Marine Force is organized into three Marine Expeditionary Forces: two for the Pacific Fleet, which is headquartered in Hawaii, and one for the Atlantic Fleet, headquartered in Norfolk, Virginia. In addition, one marine division and one marine aircraft

Women recruits at the Marine Corps Recruit Depot at Parris Island, South Carolina, receive instruction in the firing of the M-16 rifle. Women marines can be found in all fields and occupations of the corps with the exception of the combat units of the infantry, artillery, armor, and air wings.

wing are stationed in the United States and held in the Marine Corps Reserve to reinforce marine forces upon mobilization.

Each Expeditionary Force is organized into an integrated air-sea-ground unit called a Marine Air-Ground Task Force. These task forces are organized so that they can assault targets anywhere in the world amphibiously or by air. The Air-Ground Task Forces are designed to be mobile and self-contained and can be moved by sea from one trouble spot to the next to meet American security needs as they arise.

Each Air-Ground Task Force has a command element, a ground combat element, an aviation combat element, and a combat service support element (which handles logistical matters such as distributing supplies and ammunition to the combat troops). These elements can vary in size, depending on the sort of opposition the force is expected to encounter. For instance, the ground combat element can be as small as a battalion (approximately 1,600 marines). Or it can be as large as a regiment (roughly 7,000 marines) or even a division (about 20,000 marines). The ground and aviation elements of each task force are trained to work together to deliver the maximum firepower necessary for successful amphibious and airlift operations. The aviation section uses jet fighter-bombers, helicopters, and Vertical/Short Take-off and Landing planes, called V/STOLs. (V/STOLs are airplanes that can take off and land like helicopters.)

The Air-Ground Task Forces are oriented primarily to fight in what has been termed "low to medium intensity" wars, which means that the marines' primary role in the 1990s and beyond is to counter any threats to American interests in developing countries. Under this strategy the marines do not maintain a presence in Europe—although they are ready at a moment's notice to back up the army should they be needed anywhere in the region.

In order to carry out its latest role successfully, the Marine Corps must anticipate the kind of opposition it might encounter on the modern battlefield. One of the greatest threats now facing the marines comes from new technology—the so-called smart weapons that have revolutionized the modern battlefield. These weapons typically are light, highly mobile, and lethal. They are rocket-powered explosives guided by laser and computer technology that are extremely accurate from a long range and do not require a force highly trained in technological warfare to operate them. Three examples of this sort

A marine fires a Stinger antiaircraft missile during an exercise at the White Sands Missile Range in New Mexico in 1984. The Stinger is among the latest generation of weapons known as smart weapons because they are guided by laser or computer technology and do not require a force highly trained in technological warfare to operate them.

111

of weapon are the Stinger antiaircraft missile, the Exocet air-to-ground missile, and the Silkworm missile.

The Stinger, an American-made weapon, was effectively used by the Afghan guerrillas to defeat Soviet forces that had invaded Afghanistan in 1979. The Stinger can be carried and fired by a single soldier and can shoot down even the most sophisticated helicopter or airplane from several miles away. The French-manufactured Exocet missile is carried by an airplane and can sink a warship from a distance of 30 to 40 miles. Its computer-guided radar makes it very accurate, and the attacking plane can escape unharmed because of the great distance from which the missile can be launched. The Exocet was successfully used by the Argentine air force against the British navy during the Falklands War in 1982. The Silkworm missile, a Chinese weapon that can be fired from land against ships, has a range of up to 40 miles. Some of the world's poorer countries now have these types of weapons in their arsenals. If the marines are ever given the order to attack one of these countries, they must be ready with new tactics and weapons of their own to counteract this new threat to their life.

The AV-8B Harrier, a vertical takeoff and landing aircraft, gives the marines much more speed and flexibility than they previously had. The Harrier can fly more than three times as fast as a helicopter and can land in almost any type of terrain.

One of the ways the Marine Corps has responded to this relatively cheap, effective firepower has been to acquire the V/STOL AV-8B Harrier, a vertical takeoff and landing aircraft. The Harriers give the marines much more speed and flexibility than they previously had. For instance, whereas a helicopter can fly at a cruising speed of perhaps 150 miles per hour, the Harrier can attain a maximum speed of 574 miles per hour. The Harrier can take off not only from an aircraft carrier, but, unlike the airplane it is replacing, the A-4 Skyhawk, it can take off and land on a small troop-transport ship. It can even land in a clearing the size of a basketball court in places as diverse as the top of a mountain, the middle of a jungle, or in any other terrain where a small space can be cleared. This allows much greater flexibility in the marine response to forces that have accurate long-range weapons. The Marine Corps also hopes to acquire the V/STOL V-22A Osprey, a troop-transport helicopter that is still under development. The Osprey will allow the marines to fly troops to positions much faster than is now possible with helicopters.

Another piece of machinery that will boost the marines' effectiveness is the Landing Craft Air Cushion (LCAC), the most modern type of landing craft, which replaced the old World War II–vintage LCVPs. This 88-foot-long-by-47-foot-wide navy landing craft can travel at 40 knots (versus 10 knots for the old LCVPs) and is capable of landing troops from ships that are 20 to 40 miles out to sea. (Previously troop transports had to be two and a half or three miles from the beach.)

Special Services: Embassy Guards

One of the special duties of the Marine Corps is to guard U.S. embassy buildings and overseas diplomatic personnel from attack. This service was requested by the State Department after U.S. consul general T. C. Wasson was killed in a sniper attack in Jerusalem in May 1948. In 1949 the State Department and the marines reached an agreement whereby the corps would supply a small detachment of security guards depending on the circumstances at each site. Today marines provide protection to 140 embassies and consulates in 126 countries around the world.

The marine guards screen visitors to the embassy, protect the classified documents and coding machines that are found inside every embassy, and defend embassy personnel in the event of an attack on an embassy building. The guards are not armed with heavy weaponry but instead carry pistols, shotguns, and tear gas. They do not have the capacity to maintain a sustained

113

A marine stands guard atop the U.S. embassy in San Salvador, El Salvador. Marines have served as security guards at U.S. foreign posts since 1949 and today provide protection to 140 embassies and consulates around the world.

defense of American embassy buildings. Their job is to keep attackers at bay long enough to allow the local police to arrive on the scene and restore order. If the local police do not do this, often the marines cannot stop a mob from taking control of an embassy.

Marines have had to defend U.S. embassies on dozens of occasions since 1949. American embassies in Lebanon, El Salvador, and Colombia have been the target of repeated attacks, and embassies in Pakistan, Cyprus, Vietnam, Cambodia, and the Sudan have also been attacked at various times. The most well known incident of an attack on an American embassy occurred in Tehran, Iran, in 1979. On November 4 the embassy was overrun by Iranian militants. Seven marine guards fought the crowd with tear gas, but Iranian authorities did nothing to stop the mob, and eventually it broke into the building. Inside, Staff

Sergeant Michael Moeller began shredding secret documents and destroying coding equipment while the other marines slowed the advance of the attackers. The marines finally surrendered when ordered to do so by the embassy chargé d'affaires, the State Department officer in charge. Sixty-five American civilians and 13 marines were taken prisoner that day. Four marines and nine diplomats were released two weeks later. The others were held captive in Iran for 444 days, finally gaining their freedom on January 20, 1981.

Two marines raise the American flag on the SS Mayaguez, *an American cargo ship that was captured by Cambodian rebels in May 1975. Following the incident marines were ordered to the area by President Gerald Ford to rescue the ship and its crew.*

SEVEN

Leathernecks in the Age of Star Wars

Throughout its history the United States Marine Corps has shown its willingness to fight for the goals of the U.S. government. Sometimes these goals have been noble, as in the revolutionary war, the Barbary wars, and World War II. Sometimes the goals have been less than noble, as was the case in Nicaragua, Haiti, and Panama. And other times the goals have simply been unfocused, as in Korea and Vietnam.

Whatever sort of war the U.S. government has sent the marines into, the corps has proven that it has the vitality to survive technological and institutional change. It remains today what it was in 1775—an elite fighting force known for its toughness and spirit. Yet in spite of this willingness to sacrifice on the part of the marines, the world we live in is a much different place than it was in 1775 or 1848—or even in 1941—and the old gung-ho spirit can be a dangerous and simpleminded vanity in this age of revolutionary turmoil and high firepower. The United States has learned that, despite its vast nuclear arsenal, it cannot always get its way in international affairs or expect to win every war in which it engages. This is probably truer now than at any other time in the history of the country. Because the small nations of the world are armed with chemical and smart weapons and because they have seen how a guerrilla army can defeat the well-equipped and well-trained armies of the superpowers, they are no longer as willing to bend to the wishes of the great powers as they once were. For instance, after the May 1989 general election in Panama was declared fraudulent, the United States beefed up its armed forces there in an effort to pressure dictator Manuel Antonio Noriega to step down. Although more than 1,800 additional U.S. troops, including some 140 marines, were sent to Panama in the weeks following the election, this military muscle flexing did little to dislodge Noriega. The standoff between the United States and General Noriega, who was indicted on drug charges in Miami, Florida, in February 1988, left the U.S. government in an awkward position. Not wanting to draw sharp criticism from Latin American countries for intervening in Panamanian affairs, the United States was hesitant to use force to settle the issue. Yet Noriega refused to be intimidated by American military superiority and potential military action.

This is a time when the United States and the Soviet Union are just beginning to learn the limitations of their strength. Perhaps, as a result, both

Marines wade ashore at Da Nang, South Vietnam, in July 1965. In Vietnam, the United States Marine Corps showed its willingness to fight for the goals of the U.S. government, as it has throughout the corps's history.

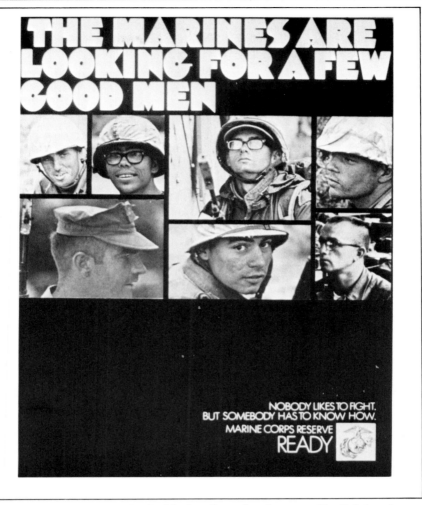

Since its inception in 1775 the Marine Corps has been an elite fighting force known for its courage and spirit. It is the conviction that they are the best and the toughest that gives the marines their strong sense of esprit de corps.

superpowers will try harder to find new ways to settle their conflicts with other nations of the world. In any event, the years ahead will be full of uncertainty as the old order falls away and the new one takes its place. As always, the marines will be ready "with a few good men" in case misunderstandings spill into war. It is the hope of all Americans that this time does not come soon—or at all.

U.S. Marine Corps
DEPARTMENT OF THE NAVY

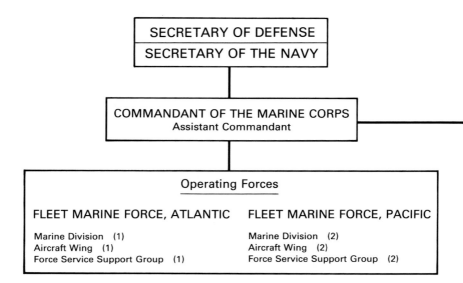

SECRETARY OF DEFENSE

SECRETARY OF THE NAVY

COMMANDANT OF THE MARINE CORPS
Assistant Commandant

Operating Forces

FLEET MARINE FORCE, ATLANTIC   FLEET MARINE FORCE, PACIFIC

Marine Division   (1)   Marine Division   (2)
Aircraft Wing   (1)   Aircraft Wing   (2)
Force Service Support Group   (1)   Force Service Support Group   (2)

Marine Corps Reserve

-Fourth Marine Division
-Fourth Marine Aircraft Wing
-Fourth Service Support Group

Supporting Establishment

Staff Judge Advocate
Chief of Staff

-Deputy Chief of Staff for Manpower and Reserve Affairs
-Deputy Chief of Staff for Installations and Logistics
-Deputy Chief of Staff for Plans, Policy, and Operations
-Deputy Chief of Staff for Aviation
-Deputy Chief of Staff for Requirements and Programs
-Assistant Chief of Staff for Command, Control, Communications, and Computer Intelligence
-Fiscal Director
-Director, Judge Advocate Division
-Legislative Assistant to the Commandant and Director of Public Affairs
-Director of Administration and Resource Management
-Director of Marine Corps History and Museum

GLOSSARY

Amphibious operation   A landing of ground forces from ships—by way of landing craft, helicopters, or aircraft—in order to defeat enemy troops and secure territory for American forces.

Fleet Marine Force   The assault unit of the U.S. Marine Corps. The Fleet Marine Force is divided into three active Marine Expeditionary Forces that are carried aboard ships of the U.S. Navy.

Landing Craft Air Cushion (LCAC)   The most advanced landing craft in the navy arsenal. The LCAC is powered by hovercraft engines that allow it to speed just above the surface of the water.

Landing Craft, Vehicle, Personnel (LCVP)   The first modern landing craft, used during World War II and the Korean War and powered by conventional nautical propeller-driven engines.

Low-intensity war   A war fought by the United States or any other technically advanced nation against a smaller, poorer nation that does not involve the use of nuclear weapons or large numbers of advanced tanks or airplanes.

Marine Air-Ground Task Force   The basic marine combat-assault unit, which uses coordinated attacks by marine airplanes and ground troops to achieve its objectives of defeating enemy forces and seizing territory.

Smart weapon   An easy-to-use, highly mobile, and technologically advanced long-range weapon (usually powered by a rocket) that can destroy an airplane, tank, or ship from a great distance.

Vertical envelopment   A marine strategy for defeating an enemy force by surrounding it with marine troops ferried to the battleground by helicopters or V/STOL airplanes.

Vertical/Short Take-off and Landing (V/STOL) airplane   An airplane that is able to take off and land like a helicopter.

SELECTED REFERENCES

Clifford, Kenneth J. *Progress & Purpose: A Developmental History of the United States Marine Corps 1900–1970.* Washington, DC: United States Marine Corps Historical and Museums Division, 1974.

Hewett, Linda. *Women Marines in World War I.* Washington, DC: United States Marine Corps Historical and Museums Divison, 1977.

Lawliss, Chuck. *The Marine Book: A Portrait of America's Military Elite.* New York: Thames and Hudson, 1988.

Lippard, Karl. *The Warriors: United States Marines.* Lancaster, TX: Vietnam Marines Publications, 1983.

Mersky, Peter. *United States Marine Corps Aviation.* Annapolis, MD: Nautical and Aviation Publishing, 1983.

Millett, Allan Reed. *Semper Fidelis: A History of the United States Marine Corps.* New York: Macmillan, 1980.

Moskin, J. Robert. *The U.S. Marine Corps Story.* New York: McGraw-Hill, 1987.

Petit, Michael. *Peacekeepers at War: A Marine's Account of the Beirut Catastrophe.* Boston: Faber & Faber, 1986.

Shaw, Henry I. *Blacks in the Marine Corps.* Washington, DC: United States Marine Corps Historical and Museums Division, 1975.

Simmons, Edwin H. "A Compilation of the Articles in the *Marine Corps Gazette,* November, 1973 through December, 1974." United States Marine Corps, 1975. Photocopy.

————. *The United States Marine Corps: 1775–1975.* New York: Viking Press, 1976.

Smith, Charles R. *Marines in the Revolution: A History of the Continental Marines in the American Revolution, 1775–1783.* Washington, DC: United States Marine Corps Historical and Museums Division, 1975.

United States Marine Corps. *180 Landings of the United States Marine Corps: 1800–1934.* Washington, DC: United States Historical and Museums Division, 1974.

United States Marine Corps. *The Marines in Vietnam.* Washington, DC: United States Marine Corps Historical and Museums Division, 1974.

INDEX

Jack Rummel is a free-lance writer who lives in Hoboken, New Jersey, and received a B.A. in history and sociology from the University of Texas. He has written for numerous publications and has contributed the volumes *Malcolm X, Langston Hughes,* and *Muhammad Ali* to the Chelsea House series BLACK AMERICANS OF ACHIEVEMENT.

Arthur M. Schlesinger, jr., served in the White House as special assistant to Presidents Kennedy and Johnson. He is the author of numerous acclaimed works in American history and has twice been awarded the Pulitzer Prize. He taught history at Harvard College for many years and is currently Albert Schweitzer professor of the Humanities at the City College of New York.

DATE			